創意燒烤

Creative Chinese Oven Cooking
The New Trend

陳雪霞 Hsueh-Hsia Chen

味全食譜
Wei-Chuan Cookbook

作者：陳雪霞
總編輯：黃淑惠
編　輯：邱澄子、陳素真
文稿協助：陳素真、官素玲、賴燕貞、何久恩、蔡壽蓮
烹飪協助：黃瓊慧、林佩怡
英文翻譯：陳寶妃、凱綠娜
設計：ZRF
攝影：林坤鴻
分色製版：福茂彩色製版有限公司
印刷：錦龍印刷實業股份有限公司
出版者：味全出版社有限公司
台北市仁愛路四段28號2樓
電話：2702-1148‧2702-1149
傳真：2704-2729
郵政劃撥00182038號
味全出版社帳戶
版權所有：局版台業字第0179號
1999年10月初版　1-0-9
2000年 4月 2版　2-1-7
定價：新台幣參佰貳拾元整

感謝： 合同興股份有限公司（鳴海骨磁）
全球餐旅開發股份有限公司
道具提供

AUTHOR: Hsueh-Hsia Chen
EDITOR: Su-Huei Huang
ASSOCIATE EDITOR: Cheng-Tzu Chiu, Su-Jen Chen
EDITORIAL STAFF: Su-Jen Chen , Su-Ling Guan ,
Yen-Jen Lai, John Holt, Shou-Lien Tsai
COOKING ASSISTANT: Chyong-Huei Huang ,
Pey-Yi Lin
ENGLISH TRANSLATION: Pao-Fei Chen ,
Rena Leaneen Kile
ART DIRECTION: ZRF
PHOTOGRAPHY: K .Lin
PRINTED IN TAIWAN

WEI-CHUAN PUBLISHING
1455 Monterey Pass Rd.,#110
Monterey Park, CA 91754, U.S.A.
TEL:(323)261-3880
FAX:(323)261-3299
Url: http://www.weichuanusa.com

FIRST PRINTING: October 1999
SECOND PRINTING: APRIL 2000
We would like to extend our appreciation
to VERSACRAFT CORPORATION and
UNIVERSAL HOTEL & RESTAURANT
SUPPLIES CO.,LTD. for supplying us with
dishes and tableware.

ISBN 0-941676-78-1

7 16598 00078 9

創意燒烤

Creative Chinese Oven Cooking

1杯
（1飯碗）
236 c.c.

1大匙
（1湯匙）
15 c.c.

1小匙
（1茶匙）
5 c.c.

CONTENTS

序

從事烹飪教學工作二十餘年，常想中國人烹飪菜餚為何這麼忙碌辛苦，而西方人烹飪菜餚卻可以這麼輕鬆簡單，廚房又乾淨，經我探討後發現，中、西烹調法和烹調用具的使用是一大原因。用烤箱來烹調不但簡單而且幾乎無油煙，烤時只要把溫度和時間設定好，食物放入烤箱後即可去做別的事情或喝杯茶，時間一到即可享受香噴噴的菜餚。

個人覺得中國菜的傳統美食聞名世界，應好好傳承，更希望因簡單化而使外國友人或海外華人也易於烹煮中國菜，所以著手研究中國菜利用烤箱來烹煮，結果發現許多的中國菜同樣可以達到美味可口的效果，就如台灣名菜「台式焢肉」，原需小火慢燒及長時間小心照顧翻拌以免燒焦，若以烤箱烹煮則方便多了。

目前報告指出，吸入過多油煙對人體有害，除了傳統的烹調外，若能取用不同烹調方式的優點，不但可以變化口味，進一步也可提昇吃的品質。

朋友常問，我在家宴客為何如此輕鬆？廚房又有條理？其實，我只是用了一些烹調技巧，譬如「鋁紙烤魚」，只要魚先調味包妥存於冰箱中，食前再送入烤箱，便可上桌和朋友聊天，不致因忙著烹煮東西而失掉宴客的意義。

烤箱食譜出書前，本人曾在家不斷的試做品嚐，期間家人反應相當好，尤其是就讀研究所的女兒特別關心何時可出書？因為她看到利用烤箱就可以輕鬆地做出這麼多美味佳餚，除了讚不絕口外，更驚呼：「媽！我以後結婚要買三部烤箱，這樣三餐就不用煩惱了。」雖是一句玩笑話，卻使我感受到這正是一本符合現代新女性簡便、快速的料理食譜。

本書大部份以中國菜為主，也取用一部分適合中國口味的改良西式菜餚與讀者分享，希望您也能成為一位輕鬆、漂亮的烹飪高手。

INSTRUCTION

Having taught cooking for more than twenty years, I always wondered why Chinese cooking took so much hard work, while Occidental cooking was easy-to-prepare and kept kitchens clean. After researching this question , I found it was the cooking methods and appliances that made the difference. Cooking foods by baking in an oven is simple and virtually smokeless. To bake, you merely set the oven temperature and time for baking then put in the food. While the food is baking, you have free time to relax, and plan on enjoying the dish after it is done.

I have consistently devoted myself to making Chinese cooking more simple to prepare while retaining the wonderful flavors and tastes. For example, the famous Taiwanese cuisine Simmered Pork, requires simmering over low heat for a long time and has to be stirred often to avoid scorching. This dish was made much easier by oven baking. Chinese cooking is popular all over the world therefore these techniques should endure for generations.

Recent reports mention that breathing oily smoke is harmful to human health. Therefore, why not take advantage of baking not only to vary taste but also reduce unhealthy, oily smoke and keep the kitchen clean?

Before this cookbook was published, I practiced these recipes at home. My family tasted and liked these dishes, especially my daughter who is studying in graduate school. She often asked me when this cookbook would be published, for she found that baking foods by oven was easier to prepare and tasted delicious. She would like to buy three ovens for cooking dinners when she is married. From her, I see that modern women who wish cooking to be simple and efficient will learn to appreciate this cookbook.

I have compiled many tasty Chinese recipes and some Occidental dishes in this book. The book describes, step-by-step and in clear detail all techniques needed to easily make a delicious feast.

現任：
★中國文化大學生活應用科學系專任講師
　從事烹飪教學27年
★實踐大學生活應用科學系兼任講師
★台灣師範大學家政教育系
　暑期中等教師餐飲班烹飪教師
★中國廣播公司烹飪主講

曾任：
★味全烹飪學校教師
★中國電視公司中國菜示範
★應菲律賓菲華文教會及德國家庭協會之邀
　前往講授中華飲食文化及中國菜示範教學
★全國技藝競賽烹飪組及多項烹飪大賽評審
★曾編著多本食譜，以如何簡化烹調為主

作者：陳 雪 霞
Hsueh-Hsia Chen

Occupations:
★ Lecturer of Home Economics at the Chinese Culture University, teaching and lecturing on Chinese cooking for 27 years.
★ Teacher of cooking classes in summer school at the National Taiwan Normal University in Taipei.
★ Lecturer of cooking programs on Chinese broadcasts.

Experiences:
★ Teacher at Wei-Chuan Cooking school.
★ Demonstrator in Chinese cooking programs on Chinese Television.
★ Guest lecturer to many foreign groups interested in the art of Chinese cookery.
★ Judge for many Chinese Cooking competitions.
★ Author of many cookbooks regarding simplified cooking steps.

烤 箱 的 使 用 方 法
OVEN COOKING HINTS

烤箱是現代化家庭非常實用的烹調用具之一。如何利用烤箱做出色、香、味俱全的佳餚,關鍵在於溫度及時間的控制,在此特別將烤箱的使用方法及烹調原則分述如下:

一、 烤箱溫度的設定

依食物的體積大小與特性來設定烤箱的溫度,才能烤出好的質地與色澤。一般大塊食物需以長時間,中、低溫(180℃/350℉)烤焙,才能將熱傳導至中心部位;若溫度太高,可能外表已烤焦,而中心又未熟。而小塊食物宜用短時間高溫(220℃/425℉)加熱,才不致內部已熟,而表面未焦化或表面焦化內部過熟,(要回烤的食物,可參照上法加熱)。由於烤箱具有不同的性質與功能, 所以建議讀者使用前應先了解自己烤箱的性能,再參考食譜來設定溫度,以達最佳效果。

華氏與攝氏的溫度之換算:

150℃=300℉	200℃=400℉
160℃=325℉	220℃=425℉
180℃=350℉	230℃=450℉
190℃=375℉	250℃=475℉

二、 烤箱預熱

預熱是指食物入烤箱前,先將烤箱加熱至所需的烤焙≧溫度,才放入食物,有如先熱鍋的意思,如魚、肉等蛋白質食物,一入烤箱即能受到高熱,以封住表面,可防肉汁流失,影響品質。一般家庭式小烤箱可於烤前15分鐘預熱,即可達預熱之效果。

The oven is one of the more practical appliances in modern households. Foods requiring long cooking times can be baked with less attention, while still achieving good flavor. Baked foods are easy to prepare. Described below is the operation of an oven and tips to get tasty and tempting dishes through baking.

I. Baking temperatures

In order to bake food with good texture and color, oven temperatures must be properly controlled. Big chunks of food, require baking at low or medium heat (180℃/350℉) for a longer time. If the temperature is too high, the food may be overcooked on the surface while uncooked inside. However, small pieces of food require baking at high temperatures (220℃/425℉) for a short time to cook well; this will not cause overcooking. (Use the same method for reheating the baked food.) To ensure the best possible flavors for prepared foods, you should follow the recipe closely while also taking the quality and function capabilities of the oven into consideration. Both of these conditions will affect the baking temperatures.

Temperature Equivalents

150℃=300℉	200℃=400℉
160℃=325℉	220℃=425℉
180℃=350℉	230℃=450℉
190℃=375℉	250℃=475℉

II. Preheating the oven

Preheat the oven before putting the food in. The heat of the preheated oven will solidify protein on the surface of the meat, avoiding the loss of desirable juices. Fifteen minutes of preheating is sufficient for small ovens.

三、 烤焙時間的設定

烤焙所需的時間，須視食物的特性、重量、厚薄、體積，以及所要烤熟的程度而不同，如帶骨的肉就比未帶骨的時間要長，厚的就比薄的時間長。通常可依經驗訂出一個平均時間，所以參考食譜外，最好能以基本的測試法來測定。可參考如下說明：

1、以香味來判定：很多食物烤熟後會有香味產生，尤其魚、 肉 類會因烤熟而產生香味。

2、烤全雞：可用竹籤或筷子插入雞腿，以流出的汁液來判斷，若流出的汁液尚有血色，表末熟；若汁液澄清，則表示已熟。

3、較厚之肉則可以色澤及軟硬度來判定熟度，食物會因加熱而變色，如蝦、肉類等。另外，如肉類熟了，會變得較硬，蔬菜熟了會變軟。

4、以鋁紙包封住燜烤者，若鋁紙鼓起則表示已熟，熟時會因蒸氣的熱度而使之膨脹。

5、讀者可依個人喜愛的熟度及焦化程度，彈性調整烘烤時間，如本食譜第26頁蒜頭雞，烤焙時間為1-1 1/2 小時，1小時表示已熟，而喜食熟透者，可延長為1 1/2 小時。

四、 烤焙位置的設定

烤箱有上、中、下層位置之設置，可依食物本身的需要來決定位置，需上火強的(如焗上色)，則必須放置在上層；需下火強的則放下層，一般則可放中層。若有上、下火控制之烤箱，則可依需要調整用上火、下火或上下火等。

III. Setting baking times

Setting times for baking depend on food characteristics, weight, thickness, size, and desired taste. For instance, meat with bone takes more time for baking than that without bone; thick materials also take more time than thin ones. The average time for baking is usually set by past experience. Whether the dish is done or not may depend on the recipes or the following tips:

1. Mostly the flavor of foods will be enhanced if cooked well. Especially for baking fish or meat, their flavors are enhanced when sufficiently cooked.

2. For baking whole chicken, perforate chicken legs with a skewer or chopsticks. If the juice coming out is clear, it's done; however, it's not cooked well if the juice is bloody.

3. The color and texture will suffer if food like thick meat is cooked insufficiently. Foods such as shrimp and meat will change color as cooked. Meat will become hard if overcooked, while vegetables become soft.

4. Foods wrapped in foil paper will become puffy due to a build up of steam. This indicates the food is sufficiently cooked.

5. Setting the time for baking foods in an oven depends on individual taste. For example, "Garlic Chicken" on p.26 takes 1- 1 1/2 hours for baking. In fact, one hour for baking the chicken is sufficient. Yet, the time may be increased by half an hour to cook more thoroughly, depending on one's personal preference.

五、 食物回烤法

食物烤熟直接食用味道最佳，但宴客時為了事先準備或有剩餘時，則必須於食用前再回烤，回烤溫度的設定，可參照食譜，其原則如下：

1、 菜餚需再烤上色者，烤箱須先預熱後再烤，如第60頁烤牛肉。

2、 色澤已夠的回烤菜餚，如第34頁烤豬肋排，則用中溫（190℃/375℉）加熱。

3、 須燜烤之菜餚，如第26頁蒜頭雞，直接送入烤箱加熱即可，或用微波爐加熱，更快速。

六、 烤焙過程注意事項

1、 烤焙時不可經常打開烤箱門，以免溫度流失而影響烤焙溫度。

2、 烤箱內的溫度不是絕對均勻，故需在適當的時間將烤盤調頭，以免有些過焦，而又有些不熟。(旋風式烤箱因熱氣循環可免)。

3、 盛裝食物之器具宜選用高溫不變質也不易破裂者。

IV. Oven rack settings

Stove ovens generally have three rack setting levels-- upper rack for upper heat, and lower rack for lower heat. Cooking on the middle rack is generally appropriate for most foods. However, the setting (upper or lower) specified in the recipe should be used for the best results. Dishes using upper heat can result in a golden brown color on the food's surface, while cooking on lower heat will absorb more heat from the bottom. If the oven is equipped with an oven heat control that can be set to "top", "bottom" or both, then the same result can be achieved by using the appropriate control setting.

V. Reheating baked foods

Serving baked foods right after they are done will allow for the best taste. For food prepared in advance or leftovers, reheating is necessary. The reheating temperature should be set according to the recipe and the following :

1. Preheat the oven before baking the fried foods to achieve a golden brown hue. See "Baked Steak" on p.60.

2. Reheat the colored foods such as "Roast Pork Ribs" on p.34 over low heat (190 ℃ /375 ℉).

3. Bake the simmering dish such as "Garlic Chicken" on p.26 in the oven or cook in the microwave for a shorter time.

VI. Directions during baking process

1. Don't open the oven door too often to avoid heat loss and lowering baking temperature.

2. Rotate the baking tray at proper intervals to avoid cooking unevenly, because heat in the oven is not constantly equal everywhere. (It's unnecessary if there is whirling air inside the oven.)

4、 鋁箔可當蓋子，用完即丟，亦可用來包封食物，可得爛烤的效果，用雙層鋁箔包可增加固定作用。

5、 材料放烤架上烤時，底下應放烤盤，並舖鋁箔紙，用來接流下的湯汁，並方便清洗。

6、 烤食物時，途中可適時塗上烤肉醬或醬汁，以防止乾澀，且可保持食物的濕潤及色澤，增加味道。

7、 不易上色的食物，可先以鍋煎至表面上色，再入烤箱烤熟，色澤容易控制，且不致因煎太久油煙太多，又怕燒焦。

七、 烤箱的使用與保養

1、 使用新烤箱時，應詳讀說明書。

2、 烤箱使用時，勿放置水槽邊或接觸冷水，以免危險。

3、 烤箱所需電流大，勿與其他電器用同插座，以防電壓負荷超過產生危險。

4、 烤箱烤焙時溫度很高，避免用手直接接觸機器或用具，可準備厚的防熱手套，以防燙傷。

5、 使用後宜趁微溫時，以紙巾擦去油漬，再以濕布擦淨內部，但不宜以水直接沖洗。

3. Cookware should be heat resistant to avoid crack or degeneration.

4. Use foil paper as a cover or to wrap foods for simmering effect, then remove after baking. In addition, wrap foods in two layers of foil paper for strength to stabilize food.

5. Cover baking tray with foil, then brush foods with oil and place them on the tray. This will keep the baking tray mess free.

6. Baste foods with sauce such as barbecue sauce during baking, not only to preserve color and moisture but also to enhance flavor.

7. Foods that are difficult to color may be fried until light brown, then baked in an oven to achieve a golden brown hue. By using these two steps, foods don't have to fry as long, therefore, less oily smoke builds up and scorching will not occur.

VII. Operation and maintenance of oven

1. Before operating an oven, read its manual thoroughly and/or read instructions on the oven door.

2. During operation, the temperature in the oven is very high. Wear thick gloves when retrieving foods to avoid burns.

3. After operation, while the oven is slightly warm, use paper towels to remove grease then damp cloth to clean inside.

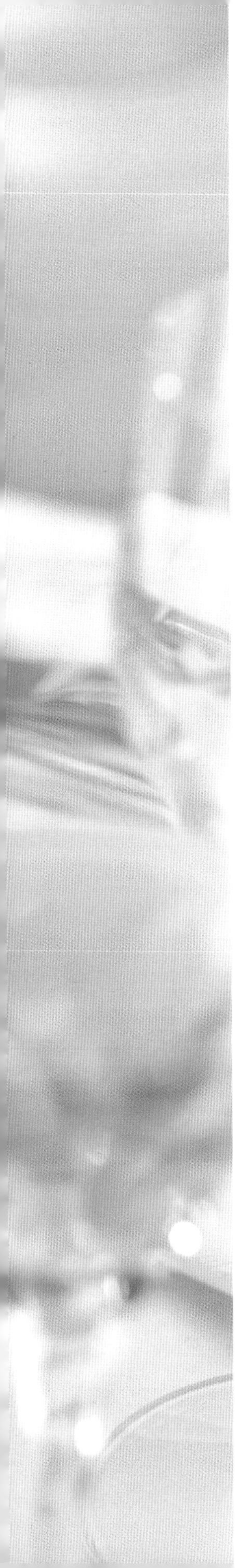

洋蔥雞
Chicken and Onions

雞腿或雞 …… 600公克（1斤）
洋蔥 ………… 225公克（6兩）

① ┌ 醬油 ………………… 3大匙
　├ 糖 ………………… ½小匙
　├ 酒 ………………… 2大匙
　└ 水 ………………… ¼杯

1 雞切塊，洋蔥切絲備用。

2 油3大匙燒熱，將洋蔥炒香，加雞塊略炒，隨入①料待滾，裝入烤盅，加蓋或以鋁箔紙包妥。

3 烤箱預熱至190℃（375°F），烤盅置中層，烤約40分鐘即可。

老師的叮嚀：

1 喜食辣味者，可加少許紅辣椒片。

2 洋蔥的香味及甜味，一直是做菜的好配料，這道洋蔥燒雞肉，以燜烤的方式來做，特別香。

1⅓ lb. (600g) chicken legs or chicken
½ lb. (225g) onions

① ┌ **3T. soy sauce**
　├ **½ t. sugar**
　├ **2T. wine**
　└ **¼ c. water**

1 Chop chicken into pieces; shred onions.

2 Heat 3T. oil and stir-fry onions until fragrant. Add chicken and stir-fry. Add ① and bring to boil; remove. Put in a baking casserole; cover or seal with foil paper.

3 Preheat oven to 190°C (375°F). Bake chicken in casserole on middle rack for 40 minutes until done; serve.

Footnotes:

1 You may add some red chili slices for a spicy accent.

2 Onions have a strong, sweet flavor as well as an unmistakable aroma. When baked with chicken, the onion aroma becomes quite irresistible.

家常雞腿
Home Style Chicken Legs

2人份／serves 2

雞腿(去骨)2隻 300公克(8兩)

① ┌ 醬油 ⋯⋯⋯⋯⋯⋯ 3大匙
　└ 糖、酒 ⋯⋯⋯⋯ 各1⅓大匙

檸檬 ⋯ 2片(或胡椒鹽適量)

1　雞腿肉攤開並在筋處稍劃開，以①料醃1小時以上或隔夜。

2　烤箱預熱至180°C(350°F)，肉放在抹油的烤架上，置中層，烤約25－30分鐘至表面呈金黃色，食時可隨喜好淋檸檬汁或撒胡椒鹽。

老師的叮嚀：

1　喜好重口味者，亦可在①料中加些蒜及辣椒。

2　雞腿取材方便，本書以雞腿做各種不同的調味應用，早上出門前醃好調味料，晚上回來時烤熟即可當主菜用，簡單又有變化。

2 boneless chicken legs, ⅔ lb. (300g)

① ┌ 3T. soy sauce
　└ 1⅓ T. each: sugar, wine

2 lemon slices or pepper salt as desired

1　Lightly cut sinew and spread chicken leg. Marinate in ① for at least 1 hour or overnight.

2　Preheat oven to 180°C (350°F). Bake chicken on greased middle rack for 25 - 30 minutes until golden brown; remove. Serve with lemon slices or pepper salt according to personal preference.

Footnotes:

1　You may also add garlic and chili in ① to enhance flavor.

2　Since chicken legs are easy to buy and are a good choice for a main dish, there are many chicken recipes in this cookbook. You may marinate chicken in the morning before going to work and bake them in the evening for dinner.

雙味雞肉串燒
Flavored Chicken Kabob

2-4人份／**Serves 2-4**

雞腿肉 ········· 300公克(8兩)	
① 青椒 紅椒 黃椒 洋蔥 ····· 共300公克(8兩)	
烤肉醬 ·············· 3大匙	
竹籤或鐵籤 ·········· 8支	
② 奶油 ·············· 1大匙 蒜末 ·············· 1小匙 胡椒、鹽 ············ 適量	

1　①料切約3公分方塊，以竹（鐵）籤串成8串。

2　依喜好刷上備好的調味料：
　　A.奶油蒜味：將肉串塗上拌勻的②料。
　　B.家常味：將肉串塗上烤肉醬。

3　烤箱預熱至200℃(400°F)，肉串放在烤架上，置中層烤約15分鐘即可。

老師的叮嚀：

1　①料可隨喜好改變，如雞肉可以豬、牛、海鮮等替代，蔬菜亦可改洋菇、鳳梨等。

2　若要保持蔬菜的色澤，可將雞肉先烤或煎至半熟再串上蔬菜。

⅔ lb. (300g) meat of chicken legs

① **total of ⅔ lb. (300g): green peppers, red peppers, yellow peppers, onions**

3T. barbecue sauce
8 skewers or wooden sticks

② **1T. butter**
1t. minced garlic
pepper and salt as desired

1　Cut ① into 1¼" (3cm) pieces then thread them equally on each skewer.

2　Brush kabob with preferred sauce:

　　A. BUTTER AND GARLIC: Brush with mixed ②.

　　B. HOME STYLE: Brush with barbecue sauce.

3　Preheat oven to 200°C (400°F). Bake kabob on middle rack for 15 minutes; serve.

Footnotes:

1　Ingredients in ① may be changed according to personal preference. For example, replace pork, beef, or seafood for chicken as well as button mushrooms or pineapples for vegetables.

2　To keep the color of vegetables, roast or fry meat until half done before threading on a skewer.

咖哩雞
Curry Chicken

① 雞腿 2 隻 …… 600 公克 (1 斤)
　馬鈴薯 (切塊) ………… 1 個
　胡蘿蔔 (切塊) ………… ½ 條
　洋蔥 (切片) ………… 1 個
　太白粉 ………… 2 大匙
　紅蔥頭 (切片) ………… 1 大匙
　咖哩粉 ………… 2 大匙
　高湯或水 ………… 2 杯
② 酒、糖 ………… 各 1 小匙
　鹽 ………… 1 小匙
③ 麵粉 ………… ½ 大匙
　水 ………… 1 大匙
④ 奶水 ………… 3 大匙
　奶油 ………… 1 大匙
　椰子粉 ………… 3 大匙

1 雞剁塊，加太白粉 2 大匙拌勻，入熱油中炸呈微黃取出，馬鈴薯亦炸片刻取出。

2 油 3 大匙燒熱，紅蔥頭以小火炸香，續炒洋蔥、咖哩粉，再入 ① 料，並加水 2 杯及 ② 料煮滾後，改中小火煮約 15 分鐘，至水約剩 1 杯時，以 ③ 料勾芡，並拌入 ④ 料，裝於烤盅，撒上椰子粉。

3 烤箱預熱至 200°C (400°F)，烤盅置中層，以上火烤約 15 分鐘至表面呈金黃色即可。

老師的叮嚀：

1 記得年輕時，曾在一家餐館吃烤過的咖哩飯，非常特別又好吃，印象非常深刻，有南國風味，又有烤的香味。

2 此道菜可先燒好後冷藏或冷凍，隨時取出烤熱即可食用。

3 烤箱若無上、下火之設置，可將烤盅放在上層烤。

① **2 chicken legs,**
　 1⅓ lb. (600g)
　 1 potato, cut in pieces
　 ½ carrot, cut in pieces
　 1 sliced onion
　 2T. cornstarch
　 1T. sliced shallot
　 2T. curry powder
　 2c. stock or water
② **1t. each: wine, sugar**
　 1t. salt
③ **½ T. flour**
　 1T. water
④ **3T. evaporated milk**
　 1T. butter
　 3T. coconut flakes

1 Chop chicken legs into pieces; mix with 2T. cornstarch. Heat oil and deep-fry chicken until light brown; remove. Then deep-fry potato for a while, remove.

2 Heat 3T. oil and deep-fry shallot over low heat until fragrant. Add onion and stir-fry. Add curry powder, ①, 2c. water, and ② then bring to boil. Reduce heat to low and cook for about 15 minutes until 1c. liquid remains. Add ③ to thicken and mix with ④; remove. Pour in a baking casserole and sprinkle with coconut flakes.

3 Preheat oven to 200°C (400°F). Use upper heat and bake chicken in casserole on middle rack for 15 minutes until golden brown ; serve.

Footnotes:

1 This dish may be prepared in advance and refrigerated; then reheated before serving.

2 If there is no control for upper heat, bake chicken legs on upper rack in the oven.

咖哩雞腿
Curry Chicken Legs

2人份／Serves 2

雞腿肉2片 … 300公克(8兩)
或雞翅 … 450公克(12兩)

① ┌咖哩粉 ………………… 1大匙
　│酒 ……………………… 1大匙
　│鹽 ……………………… ½小匙
　│糖、蒜末 ………… 各1小匙
　└胡椒 ………………… 適量

1 雞腿肉與①料拌勻，醃約1小時，雞皮朝上，置抹油的烤架上。
2 烤箱預熱至180°C(350°F)，雞肉置中層，烤約25－30分鐘至表面呈金黃色，皮脆肉熟即可。

老師的叮嚀：

1 雞腿肉醃上咖哩粉，再入烤箱烤，記得將雞皮朝上，因皮帶有油質，烤後有酥脆感，特別香。
2 咖哩粉是由許多香料組成，香味特別好，老少咸宜。

2 boneless chicken legs, ⅔ lb. (300g) or 1lb. (450g) chicken wings

① ┌**1T. curry powder**
　│**1T. wine**
　│**½ t. salt**
　│**1t. each: sugar, minced garlic**
　└**pepper as desired**

1 Mix chicken with ① and marinate for about 1 hour. Place chicken on greased rack with skin face up.
2 Preheat oven to 180°C (350°F). Place chicken on middle rack and bake for 25-30 minutes until done as well as golden brown and crisp on the surface; serve.

Footnotes:

1 Make sure to bake chicken piece with skin face up. Because the skin contains fat, it is crisp and aromatic after baking.
2 Curry powder is made of many spices so its flavor is unique and full.

九層塔雞翅
Chicken Wings and Basil

4 人份／serves 4

雞翅（中段）12 支
.... 450 公克（12 兩）

① ┌ 蒜末、辣椒末 ...... 各 1 大匙
  └ 九層塔末 .... 2 大匙

② ┌ 醬油 .... ¼ 杯
  └ 糖、醋 .... 各 1 大匙

1 雞翅洗淨，拭乾水份，以①、②料醃泡 2 小時以上或隔夜。
2 烤箱預熱至 190℃（375℉），雞翅放在抹油的烤架上，置中層，烤約 20－25 分鐘至熟且呈金黃色即可。

老師的叮嚀：
1 此道菜宜選肉雞，肉質較嫩，亦可用雞腿肉替代。

1lb. (450g) chicken wings, middle part (about 12)

① ┌ **1T. each (minced): garlic, chili**
  └ **2T. minced basil leaves**

② ┌ **¼ c. soy sauce**
  └ **1T. each: sugar, vinegar**

1 Rinse chicken wings and pat dry. Marinate in mixtures ① and ② for at least 2 hours or overnight.
2 Preheat oven to 190°C (375°F). Bake chicken wings on greased middle rack for 20 - 25 minutes until done and golden brown; serve.

Footnote:
1 Chicken legs may be substituted for wings.

鹽焗雞
Salty Chicken

雞½隻…… 約600公克(1斤)

① ⎡ 鹽 ………………………… ½大匙
　 ｜ 醬油 ……………………… 2大匙
　 ⎣ 酒 ………………………… 2大匙

② ⎡ 八角 ……………………… 1朵
　 ｜ 桂皮 ……………………… 2片
　 ｜ 蔥 ………………………… 2支
　 ｜ 薑 ………………………… 2片
　 ⎣ 芫荽莖 …………………… 3支

鋁箔紙(50公分×50公分) 2張

1 雞洗淨拭乾，以①料及②料醃拌1小時以上。

2 鋁紙中間抹油，擺上②料及雞，雞皮朝上包妥。

3 烤箱預熱至190°C(375°F)，雞置烤架上，烤約40分鐘，掀開鋁紙續烤約15分鐘至稍呈金黃色即可。

老師的叮嚀：

1 鹽焗雞是廣東名菜，利用烤箱來焗，亦非常香而肉嫩。

2 雞應待涼再剁塊，否則易散開，亦可改用雞腿來烤。

½ chicken, 1⅓ lb. (600g)

① ⎡ ½ T. salt
　 ｜ 2T. soy sauce
　 ⎣ 2T. wine

② ⎡ 1 star anise
　 ｜ 2 slices of cinnamon
　 ｜ 　 sticks
　 ｜ 2 green onions
　 ｜ 2 ginger root slices
　 ⎣ 3 coriander stems

2 aluminum foil sheets,
　 20" × 20" (50cm × 50cm)

1 Rinse chicken and pat dry. Marinate in mixtures ① and ② for at least 1 hour.

2 Rub oil on middle part of foil paper. Place ② and chicken with skin face up; fold foil closed.

3 Preheat oven to 190°C (375°F). Bake chicken on the rack for about 40 minutes. Open up foil paper and roast for another 15 minutes until lightly golden brown; serve.

Footnotes:

1 This is a famous Cantonese dish. Baking in an oven will achieve the same flavor and tenderness.

2 Chop chicken after it becomes cool or it will crumble. Chicken legs may also be used as a substitute.

五彩封雞腿
Chicken Legs and Vegetables

2人份／serves 2

雞腿肉2片 …… 450公克(12兩)

① ┌ 鹽 ……………………… ½小匙
   │ 酒、醬油……………… 各1大匙
   │ 胡椒 …………………… 適量
   └ 糖 … 1小匙，蒜末 … 1大匙

② ┌ 洋蔥絲，火腿絲
   │ 香菇絲 …………………… 1-2杯
   │ 熟筍絲，胡蘿蔔絲 ┘
   └ 太白粉 ………………… 2大匙

鋁箔紙(30公分×20公分) … 2張

1 雞腿肉以①料醃約1小時。

2 雞腿攤開，撒上太白粉，包入½的②料，捲起包成雞腿狀，置抹油的鋁紙上，將雞腿包緊。

3 烤箱預熱至180℃（350°F），雞腿置中層，烤約25分鐘後，掀開鋁紙再以200℃(400°F)烤約10分鐘至呈金黃色即可取出，待冷切片排盤。

老師的叮嚀：

1 ②料可依喜好改變或增減。

2 烤後宜稍待冷再切片，才不致鬆散。

2 boneless chicken legs,
  1lb. (450g)

① ┌ ½ t. salt
   │ 1T. each: wine, soy sauce
   │ pepper as desired
   └ 1t. sugar, 1T. minced garlic

② ┌ total of 1-2c. (shredded):
   │ onion, ham, black
   │ mushrooms, canned or
   │ cooked bamboo shoots,
   │ carrot
   └ 2T. cornstarch

2 aluminum foil sheets,
  12" × 8" (30cm × 20cm)

1 Marinate chicken legs in ① for about 1 hour.

2 Spread meat and sprinkle with cornstarch. Put ½ of ② on each leg and roll to original shape. Wrap each leg tightly in greased foil paper.

3 Preheat oven to 180°C (350°F). Bake chicken on middle rack for 25 minutes. Open foil paper and bake at 200°C (400°F) for another 10 minutes until golden brown; remove. When cool, slice and serve.

Footnotes:

1 Ingredients in ② may be changed according to personal preference.

2 Slice baked chicken legs with vegetables when it is cool to prevent falling apart.

香辣小翅腿
Spicy Chicken Wings

4人份／serves 4

雞翅上腿12隻　600公克(1斤)

① ┌ 辣椒粉　……　1小匙 － 1大匙
　├ 番茄醬　………………　2大匙
　├ 糖　………………………　½大匙
　└ 麻油、醬油、蒜末…　各1大匙

1　雞翅腿以 ① 料醃3小時以上或隔夜。
2　烤箱預熱至190℃(375℉)，雞翅放在抹油的烤架上，置中層烤約25分鐘至熟並呈金黃色即可。

老師的叮嚀：

1　辣椒粉可隨喜好增減。
2　雞翅可改用雞胸肉，但在加醃料前，一定要先拭乾水份再醃，較易入味。

12 chicken wings, upper part

① ┌ 1t. - 1T. chili powder
　├ 2T. ketchup
　├ ½ T. sugar
　└ 1T. each: sesame oil, soy sauce, minced garlic

1　Marinate chicken wings in ① for at least 3 hours or overnight.
2　Preheat oven to 190°C (375°F). Bake wings on greased middle rack for 25 minutes until golden brown and done; serve.

Footnotes:

1　The amount of chili powder may be changed according to personal preference.
2　Chicken breast may replace wings. Rinse and pat dry before marinating to enable the sauce to adhere to the chicken.

三杯雞
Three Sauce Chicken

雞半隻 … 約900公克(1½斤)
醬油 …………………… 1大匙
麻油 …………………… ¼杯

① ┌ 薑片 ………………… 10片
　 └ 蒜(去皮) …………… 10瓣

紅辣椒(切片) ………… 1支

② ┌ 酒 …………………… ¼杯
　 ├ 醬油 ………………… ¼杯
　 └ 糖 …………………… 2小匙

九層塔 ………………… 適量

1 雞洗淨剁塊，拭乾水分，加1大匙醬油拌勻。

2 麻油燒熱，將 ① 料爆香，隨入辣椒，雞塊炒拌至外表微黃，入 ② 料煮滾，裝入烤盅，上蓋。

3 烤箱預熱至200℃(400°F)，燜烤約40分鐘至熟，拌入九層塔即可。

老師的叮嚀：

1 三杯雞亦是頗受大家喜愛的一道佳餚，以烤箱來做味道更香又易於照顧。

2 亦可直接在烤盅中爆香、煮滾，入烤箱後傳熱更快。

3 若喜歡焦香者，亦可在烤好前10-15分鐘掀開蓋子，再烤至稍呈焦色即可。

4 九層塔有特殊之香味，但不宜太早放入，以免變軟變色。

½ chicken, about
　2 lb. (900g)
1T. soy sauce
¼ c. sesame oil

① ┌ **10 ginger root slices**
　 └ **10 peeled garlic cloves**

1 sliced red chili

② ┌ **¼ c. wine**
　 ├ **¼ c. soy sauce**
　 └ **2t. sugar**

fresh basil as desired

1 Rinse chicken and chop in pieces. Pat dry and mix with 1T. soy sauce.

2 Heat sesame oil and stir-fry ① until fragrant. Add red chili and chicken; stir-fry until chicken becomes light brown. Add mixture ② and bring to a simmer; pour in a casserole and cover.

3 Preheat oven to 200°C (400°F). Bake chicken for 40 minutes until done. Mix in fresh basil and serve.

Footnotes:

1 This is a popular dish. By baking it, it is easy to prepare as well as tasty.

2 In step 2, heat sesame oil and stir-fry materials in order directly in a casserole and bring to a simmer to reduce the baking time.

3 For a roasted flavor, open the lid 10-15 minutes before done and bake until nearly scorched.

4 Don't add in fresh basil too early or it will become wilted and discolored.

蒜頭雞
Garlic Chicken

雞1隻………　1200公克(2斤)
蒜頭（去皮）………　¼ – ½ 杯
鹽 ………………………　1大匙
酒 ………………………　¼ 杯
鋁箔紙(50公分×50公分)　2張

1 雞以滾水川燙後，取出於雞身內外均勻抹上鹽及酒。將蒜頭塞入雞肚，以雙層鋁箔紙包妥。

2 烤箱預熱至200°C(400°F)，雞放在烤盤上，置中層，烤約1－1½小時(視個人喜好的熟度增減)即可。

老師的叮嚀：

1 蒜頭雞是土雞城的名菜。

2 改用烤箱的燜烤方式，有如土窯雞，肉酥爛，蒜又香，真的非常好吃。

3 我們常吃的土窯雞亦可以此法來做，時間隨喜好的熟度增減。

1 chicken, 2⅔ lb. (1200g)
¼ - ½ c. garlic, peeled
1T. salt
¼ c. wine
2 aluminum foil sheets,
　20" × 20" (50cm × 50cm)

1 Blanch chicken in boiling water; remove. Rub salt and wine outside and inside of chicken. Stuff with garlic and wrap chicken in two layers of aluminum foil.

2 Preheat oven to 200°C (400°F). Put chicken on tray and bake on middle rack of oven for 1 - 1½ hours until done. The baking time depends on the individual's taste.

Footnote:

1 The famous Chinese dish, Baked Chicken in Soil Kiln, may be cooked by the same method as well, to achieve the same good taste.

糖果雞肉
Candy Shaped Chicken

4-8 人份／serves 4-8

雞胸肉 ⋯⋯ 450公克(12兩)

① ┌ 醬油 ⋯⋯⋯⋯⋯⋯⋯ 3大匙
　　│ 糖、芝麻 ⋯⋯⋯⋯ 各2大匙
　　│ 酒 ⋯⋯⋯⋯⋯⋯⋯⋯ 1大匙
　　│ 蒜末 ⋯⋯⋯ ½大匙(或隨意)
　　│ 胡椒粉 ⋯⋯⋯⋯⋯⋯ ¼小匙
　　└ 太白粉 ⋯⋯⋯⋯⋯⋯ 2大匙

鋁箔紙(15公分×10公分) 24張

1 雞胸肉去皮，切成5公分之長條狀，拌入 ① 料醃約1小時。

2 鋁紙攤開，擺上雞肉包成糖果狀，置烤盤上（封口向上，以免湯汁流失）。

3 烤箱預熱至200℃(400°F)，置中層，烤約15分鐘即可。

老師的叮嚀：

1 這道菜可事先準備，非常適合大型茶會、自助餐或家庭宴客用。

2 若無烤箱亦可改用蒸的方式烹製。

1lb. (450g) chicken breast

① ┌ **3T. soy sauce**
　　│ **2T. each: sugar, sesame seeds**
　　│ **1T. wine**
　　│ **½ T. minced garlic or as desired**
　　│ **¼ t. pepper**
　　└ **2T. cornstarch**

24 aluminum foil sheets, 6" × 4" (15cm × 10cm)

1 Skin chicken breast and cut into 2" (5cm) strips. Marinate in ① for about 1 hour.

2 Spread each foil sheet and put on chicken; wrap to form a "wrapped candy". Place on baking tray with sealed side up to avoid loss of juices.

3 Preheat oven to 200°C (400°F). Bake wrapped chicken on middle rack for 15 minutes until done; serve.

Footnotes:

1 This dish may be made in advance and is suitable for banquet, buffet, or party snacks.

2 If oven is not available, steaming may be substituted for baking.

東坡肉
Glazed Pork Belly

較瘦五花肉　900公克 (1½斤)

① ┌ 蔥　……………………… 6支
　├ 薑(稍拍)1塊 … 75公克 (2兩)
　├ 八角　…………………… 2朵
　└ 肉桂　…………………… 1支

② ┌ 紹興酒　………………… 2杯
　├ 醬油　……………………… ¾杯
　├ 冰糖　…………………… 3大匙
　└ 水　……………………… 2杯

1 五花肉切約6公分方塊，約可切成八塊，以綿繩綁好（以防酥爛時鬆散），入滾水中川燙一下取出。

2 取烤盅，將 ① 料排於底部，上擺肉塊（皮朝上）加②料，以鋁紙蓋妥。

3 烤箱預熱至190°C (375°F)，烤盅置中層，烤約2-3小時即可（將湯汁先煮滾再入烤箱，可縮短烤的時間約30分鐘）。

老師的叮嚀：

1 東坡肉為中國名菜，有紹興酒的醇香及慢燉的酥香，如無紹興酒，可以米酒替代。

2 此道菜平時可先做好存於冰箱，隨時加熱食用，湯汁亦可澆飯、麵等。

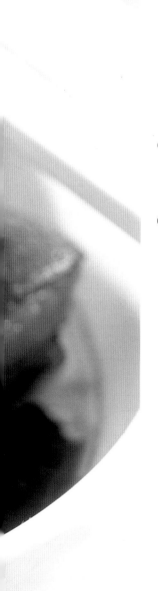

2 lb. (900g) lean pork belly

① ┌ **6 green onions**
　├ **1 crushed ginger root,**
　│　**2½ oz. (75g)**
　├ **2 star anises**
　└ **1 cinnamon stick**

② ┌ **2c. Shao Hsing rice wine**
　├ **¾ c. soy sauce**
　├ **3T. rock sugar**
　└ **2c. water**

1 Cut pork in 2.5" × 2.5" (6cm×6cm) cubes, about 8 pieces. Tie with cotton threads to prevent falling apart while cooking. Blanch in boiling water; remove.

2 Arrange ① on bottom of the casserole dish. Add pork cubes, skin side up and sprinkle on ②. Cover with foil paper.

3 Preheat oven to 190°C (375°F). Bake pork in casserole dish on middle rack for 2-3 hours until done; serve. (Boiling first may reduce baking time by 30 minutes.)

Footnotes:

1 This is a famous Chinese dish. If Shao Hsing rice wine is not available, substitute with rice wine.

2 This dish may be cooked and saved in a refrigerator. When necessary, reheat and serve at any time. The remaining sauce goes well with rice or noodles.

蒜烤豬排
Roast Pork Chops and Garlic　　2人份／**serves 2**

豬排肉2片 … 300公克(8兩)
①
┌醬油 ················· 3大匙
│糖 ················· 2小匙
│蒜末、酒 ········· 各1大匙
└胡椒 ················· ¼小匙
檸檬 ················· 2片

1 豬排用刀背或搥肉器搥鬆，以 ① 料醃1小時以上或隔夜。
2 烤箱預熱至200℃(400℉)，將豬排放在抹油的烤架上，置中層烤約15分鐘，至肉熟即可取出，灑上檸檬汁。

老師的叮嚀：

1 肉排宜烤至剛熟，肉保水而有彈性，最美味。
2 煎豬排非常好吃，若改用烤的，可避免燒焦，且可減少油煙。
3 亦可用碳火烤，味道亦佳。

2 pork chops, ⅔ lb. (300g)
①
┌3T. soy sauce
│2t. sugar
│1T. each: minced garlic,
│　　wine
└¼ t. pepper
2 lemon slices

1 Tenderize pork by pounding with the dull edge of a cleaver or a meat mallet. Marinate in ① for over 1 hour or overnight.
2 Preheat oven to 200°C (400°F). Grease middle rack of oven and roast pork for 15 minutes until done; remove. Sprinkle with lemon juice and serve.

Footnotes:

1 Roast pork chops until done and remove immediately for best flavor and texture.
2 Roasting rather than frying pork will not only reduce oily smoke but also avoid scorching.
3 Pork may also be barbecued over charcoal for better taste.

烤豬肋排
Roast Pork Ribs

4人份／serves 4

豬肋排 ……… 600公克（1斤）

① ┌ 黑胡椒醬 …………… 3大匙
│ 番茄醬 ……………… 5大匙
│ 芥末醬（圖1） ……… 1大匙
│ 醋 …………………… 1大匙
│ 蜂蜜 ………………… 1大匙
│ Tabasco（圖2）或辣椒醬 ½小匙
│ 鹽 ………………… ½小匙
│ 蒜末 ………………… 2大匙
│ 橄欖油 ……………… 2大匙
└ 酒 ………………… 2大匙

1 豬肋排在肋骨間隔處稍劃開，肉厚處亦可劃刀，以拌勻的 ① 料醃2小時以上或隔夜。

2 烤箱預熱至190℃（375°F），肉厚之一面朝上，放在抹油的烤架上，置中層，烤約45分鐘至稍呈金黃色即可（可隨時刷上剩餘之調味汁，以防乾涩）。

■ Tabasco辣椒汁：是由紅辣椒混合白醋，儲藏在橡木桶內三年釀造而成，有獨特的酸辣味，可做沾醬或醃料。

■ 法式芥末醬：是由芥末子或芥末粉為主要材料，加上鹽及香料調配而成的膏狀調味料，色黃，帶有特殊之辛辣味，可當各式肉類、香腸等之沾料，亦可當醃料或做沙拉醬時使用。

老師的叮嚀：

1 在美式餐廳，非常熱門的一道菜即是「燒烤豬肋排」，口味頗受大家的喜愛，不妨試試。

2 豬肋排帶骨，肉質帶有筋及肥肉，較有彈性，若先烤熟置於冰箱中，於食前再加熱亦非常可口。

**1 slab of pork ribs,
   1⅓ lb. (600g)**

① ┌ **3T. black pepper sauce**
│ **5T. ketchup**
│ **1T. mustard sauce (Fig.1)**
│ **1T. vinegar**
│ **1T. honey**
│ **½ t. Tabasco (Fig.2) or
│   chili sauce**
│ **½ t. salt**
│ **2T. minced garlic**
│ **2T. olive oil**
└ **2T. wine**

1 Make cuts between ribs and on thick meat part. Marinate in mixture ① for at least 2 hours or overnight.

2 Preheat oven to 190°C (375°F). Roast ribs, thick meat side up, on greased middle rack for 45 minutes until golden brown (While roasting, brush on the remaining marinade to avoid dryness).

■ Tabasco Chili Sauce: Made by mixing red chili and vinegar, then fermented in oak barrels for 3 years. The sauce is sour and spicy; used as dipping sauce or marinade.

■ French Style Mustard Sauce: Made with mustard seeds or powder mixed with salt and spices. It is yellow and spicy; usually used as salad dressing, marinade or dipping sauce for meat or sausages.

Footnotes:

1 This dish is popular in American restaurants as "Roast Country-style Ribs".

2 Pork ribs containing bones, sinew, and fat have an elastic texture. They may be roasted in advance, refrigerated, then reheated before serving; the flavor will be enhanced.

（圖1）   （圖2）

醬汁烤小排
Barbecued Spareribs

小排骨(切成4長條)
·················· 600公克(1斤)
味全烤肉醬 ⋯ ½瓶(約½杯)

1 小排骨加烤肉醬醃隔夜（要翻面）。

2 醃好之排骨置烤盅，肉厚部分朝上，以鋁紙蓋妥。

3 烤箱預熱至180°C（350°F），烤盅置中層，烤約2小時後，掀開鋁紙，再烤約15分鐘（可邊烤邊淋肉汁），至稍呈金黃色即可。

老師的叮嚀：

1 宜選帶有肥肉之肋排。

2 烤的時間，可視個人喜好之熟度增減。

3 此道菜非常美味，適合當便當菜。

4 亦可分別以鋁箔紙包妥烤熟。

1⅓ lb. (600g) spareribs, cut in 4 sections
½ bottle of Wei-Chuan Barbecue Sauce, about ½ c.

1 Marinate spareribs in barbecue sauce overnight (turning them over occasionally).

2 Put marinated spareribs in baking casserole, with thick meat side up. Cover with foil paper.

3 Preheat oven to 180°C (350°F). Bake spareribs in casserole on middle rack for 2 hours. Open foil paper and roast for another 15 minutes (pour marinade on spareribs occasionally) until golden brown; serve.

Footnotes:

1 Choose spareribs with fat.

2 The baking time may be changed according to desired doneness.

3 This is a good dish for box lunches.

4 Spareribs may also be wrapped separately in foil sheets and baked until done.

五香肉燥
Five-Spice Meat Sauce

豬絞肉 ……… 600公克(1斤)
紅蔥頭(切片) ………… ¼杯
(或炸香紅蔥頭)
蒜泥 ……………… 3大匙
酒 ……………… 2大匙

① ┌ 五香粉 ……………… 1小匙
│ 胡椒粉 …………… ½小匙
│ 糖 …………… 1⅓大匙
│ 味精 …………… ½小匙
│ 醬油 …………… ¾杯
└ 水 …………… 2杯

白煮蛋 ……………… 5個

1 油4大匙燒至五分熱，入紅蔥片以小火慢炸至金黃色後取出，餘油炒香蒜泥，並入絞肉炒鬆，加酒炒片刻，再拌入 ① 料及白煮蛋煮滾後，裝入烤盅，加蓋或以鋁紙蓋妥。

2 烤箱預熱至200°C(400°F)，烤盅置中層，燜烤約1－1½小時即可。

老師的叮嚀：

1 一家燒肉萬家香，尤其是肉燥，愈燒愈香，拌麵、拌飯、拌菜，人人喜愛。

2 燒肉必須用小火且要小心照顧，以防燒焦，如利用烤箱的間接加熱法及溫度的控制，慢慢燜烤極為方便，您不妨試著做做看。

1⅓ lb. (600g) ground pork
¼ c. shallot slices
(or ready-fried shallot)
3T. garlic paste
2T. wine

① ┌ 1t. five-spice powder
│ ½ t. pepper
│ 1⅓ T. sugar
│ ¾ c. soy sauce
└ 2c. water

5 boiled eggs

1 Heat 4T. oil to medium heat. Deep-fry shallot over low heat until golden brown; remove. In remaining oil stir-fry garlic until fragrant. Add pork and stir-fry to separate; add wine and stir-fry for a while. Add ① and eggs then bring to boil; remove. Put in a baking casserole; cover or seal with foil paper.

2 Preheat oven to 200°C (400°F). Place casserole on middle rack and bake for 1 - 1½ hours until done; serve.

Footnotes:

1 This dish goes well with rice, noodles, or boiled vegetables.

2 Baking rather than simmering, the dish is easy to prepare and is difficult to scorch.

豆豉排骨
Spareribs and Fermented Beans 4人份／serves 4

小排骨 ……… 600公克(1斤)

① ┌ 酒 …………………… ½大匙
　　├ 醬油 ………………… 2大匙
　　├ 糖 …………………… 1小匙
　　├ 麻油 ………………… 1大匙
　　└ 太白粉 ……………… 1小匙

② ┌ 豆豉 ………………… 2大匙
　　├ 薑、蒜末 ………… 各1大匙
　　├ 蔥末 ………………… 2大匙
　　└ 紅辣椒(切片) ………… 1支

1 將小排骨剁約3公分之塊狀，先拌入 ① 料，再加入 ② 料拌勻，裝入烤盅，上蓋或以鋁紙封妥。

2 烤箱預熱至200°C(400°F)，烤盅置中層，烤約1小時即可。

老師的叮嚀：

1 豆豉排骨是中國的名菜，豆豉的醱酵香味，融入排骨中，特別香醇。

2 此道菜傳統是以蒸的方式做，若身在國外或想改變烹調方式，用燜烤的方式來做，一樣非常好吃。

3 亦可以鋁紙分別包成四份來烤，食時更方便，時間可依個人喜歡的熟爛度增減。

1⅓ lb. (600g) spareribs

① ┌ **½ T. wine**
　　├ **2T. soy sauce**
　　├ **1t. sugar**
　　├ **1T. sesame oil**
　　└ **1t. cornstarch**

② ┌ **2T. fermented black beans**
　　├ **1T. each (minced) : ginger root, garlic**
　　├ **2T. minced green onions**
　　└ **1 sliced red chili**

1 Chop spareribs into 1¼" (3cm) pieces. Mix in ① then add ②. Put in baking casserole; cover or seal with foil paper.

2 Preheat oven to 200°C (400°F). Place casserole on middle rack and bake for 1 hour until done; serve.

Footnotes:

1 This is a famous Chinese dish. Traditionally it is cooked by steaming; yet, by baking it is easily prepared as well as tasty.

2 You may divide spareribs into four parts and wrap each part in foil paper. Then directly bake in oven before serving. The baking time may be changed according to desired tenderness.

紅糟肉
Crimson Pork

（圖1）

較瘦五花肉 … 600公克（1斤）

① ⎰ 蒜頭（拍碎）……………… 5瓣
醬油 ………………… 2大匙
糖 …………………… 2大匙
紅糟（圖1）………… 3大匙
味精 …………………… 隨意

1 五花肉去皮，切約2公分厚之長片狀，加①料醃2小時以上或隔夜。

2 烤箱預熱至180℃（350°F），肉放在烤架上，置中層，烤約35分鐘至熟，且表皮酥脆即可，食用時切片，可與青蒜配食。

■ 紅糟：係由米、鹽、紅麴及調味料等釀造而成，為膏狀，色紅，並帶有特殊香味之醬料，為中國福州菜常用之調味料，可用來醃製或烹煮魚、肉類。

老師的叮嚀：

1 紅糟肉是福建名菜，市場上常見用炸的，改為烤箱烤不油膩、又方便，味道更香，吃了還想再吃。

2 紅糟味道若太鹹，則可酌予減量。

1⅓ lb. (600g) lean pork belly

① ⎰ 5 garlic cloves, crushed
2T. soy sauce
2T. sugar
3T. red fermented wine rice (Fig.1)

1 Skin pork belly and slice in ¾" (2cm) thick. Marinate in ① for at least 2 hours or overnight.

2 Preheat oven to 180°C (350°F). Roast pork on middle rack for 35 minutes until done and crisp on the surface. Slice and serve with fresh garlic.

■ Red Fermented Wine Rice: Made of rice, wine, and red ferment ("An ka"). It is a red paste with a unique flavor; frequently used in Fu Chou dishes. It is also used in marinating or cooking fish and meat.

Footnotes:

1 This dish is popular in Fukien Province. Ready-made crimson pork is deep-fried. Here it is made by roasting for ease of preparation and a reduction of oil.

2 Reduce the amount of red fermented wine rice if taste is too salty.

叉燒肉
Cantonese Style Roast Pork

豬後（前）腿肉 600公克（1斤）

① ⎰ 鹽 …… 1小匙，糖 … 3大匙
醬油 … 2大匙，酒 … 2大匙
五香粉 ……………… ½小匙
食用紅色素 …………… 隨意
蒜頭（拍碎）………… 5瓣
蔥（稍拍）…………… 2支

1 肉去皮，切約2公分厚之長片狀，加①料醃2小時以上或隔夜。

2 烤箱預熱至180℃（350°F），肉放烤架上，置中層烤約35分鐘至熟即可。

老師的叮嚀：

1 烤完後外表可刷少許蜂蜜，色澤較亮又不乾澀。

2 叉燒肉是廣東名菜，也頗受大家喜愛，自己烤方便又衛生。

3 可與大蒜片配食，特別香。

1⅓ lb. (600g) pork round

① ⎰ ½ t. salt, 3T. sugar
2T. soy sauce, 2T. wine
½ t. five-spice powder
red food coloring as desired
5 garlic cloves, crushed
2 green onions, lightly crushed

1 Skin pork and cut into ¾" (2cm) thick slices. Marinate pork in ① for at least 2 hours or overnight.

2 Preheat oven to 180°C (350°F) and roast pork on middle rack for 35 minutes until done; serve.

Footnotes:

1 Brush a little honey on the surface after roasting to enhance color and taste.

2 This is a famous and popular Cantonese dish. Baking this way makes it easy to prepare and clean.

3 Serving with garlic slices adds a delicious accent.

佛跳牆
Spareribs Stewed with Taro

① 芋頭 ……… 450公克(12兩)
　 小排骨 ……… 225公克(6兩)
　 熟豬肚 ……… 150公克(4兩)
　 香菇(泡軟) ……………… 5朵
　 干貝(泡軟) ……………… 2個
　 鮑魚1個 …… 150公克(4兩)

② 酒 ………………………… 2大匙
　 鹽、糖 …………… 各1小匙
　 醬油 ……………………… 1½大匙
　 高湯或水 ……………… 4杯

1 芋頭切滾刀塊,小排骨切3公分段,分別入熱油中炸香取出,豬肚切片。
2 將①料裝入較深之烤盅,加上②料。
3 烤箱預熱至190℃(375℉),烤盅置底層,燜烤約2-3小時即可(亦可先煮滾,則烤的時間可縮短30分鐘)。

老師的叮嚀:

1 材料可依喜好改變或增減,如豬腳、魚翅、栗子、金針等皆可。
2 這是一道久燉的菜餚,以烤箱來做方便又好吃。

---

① 1lb. (450g) taro
　 ½ lb. (225g) spareribs
　 ⅓ lb. (150g) cooked pig
　　 tripe
　 5 pre-softened Chinese
　　 black mushrooms
　 2 dried scallops, pre-
　　 softened in cold water
　 1 abalone, ⅓ lb. (150g)

② 2T. wine
　 1t. each: salt, sugar
　 1½ T. soy sauce
　 4c. stock or water

1 Cut taro into cubes and cut spareribs in 1¼" (3cm) pieces. Deep-fry separately in hot oil until fragrant; remove. Slice pig tripe.
2 Put ① in a deep baking bowl; add in ②.
3 Preheat oven to 190°C (375°F). Bake all on bottom rack for about 2-3 hours until done; serve.(Boiling before baking will reduce cooking time by 30 minutes.)

Footnotes:

1 You may substitute ingredients in ① for other materials as desired, such as pork legs, shark's fins, chestnuts, or lily flowers.
2 This dish takes a long time to cook. Baking rather than frying allows it to be tasty as well as easy to prepare.

滷豬腳
Simmered Pig's Feet

豬腳(切塊)···		1200公克(2斤)
┌ 蒜頭(去皮)	·············	5瓣
│ 八角	·············	2朶
│ 醬油	·············	1杯
① 酒	·············	½杯
│ 冰糖	·············	3大匙
│ 黑醋	·············	1大匙
└ 水	·············	5杯

1 豬腳洗淨，入滾水中川燙取出，將表皮除毛並刮洗乾淨。
2 豬腳裝入烤盅，加①料煮滾，上蓋備烤。
3 烤箱預熱至190℃(375°F)，烤盅置底層，烤約2-3小時至所需熟爛度即可。

老師的叮嚀：

1 豬腳含有膠質，需小火慢煮，才會香Q好吃，用烤箱燜烤非常適合。
2 喜好酥皮者，亦可於烤好前15分鐘掀開蓋子續烤至稍呈焦色。

2⅔ lb. (1200g) chopped pig's feet

- 5 peeled garlic cloves
- 2 star anises
- 1c. soy sauce
- ① ½ c. wine
- 3T. rock sugar
- 1T. black vinegar
- 5c. water

1 Rinse pig's feet and blanch in boiling water; remove. Scrape hair from the skin and rinse.
2 Put pig's feet and ① in a baking casserole and bring to boil; cover and turn off heat.
3 Preheat oven to 190°C (375°F). Bake pig's feet in casserole on bottom rack for 2-3 hours until cooked thoroughly; serve.

Footnotes:

1 Pig's feet contains gelatin, and requires cooking over low heat for a longer period of time to achieve best taste and texture. Therefore, baking in an oven is suitable.
2 For crisp skin, remove lid 15 minutes before done and roast until the surface is nearly scorched.

台式焢肉
Taiwanese Simmered Pork

五花肉(或胛心肉)		
	·············	1200公克(2斤)
蒜頭(稍拍)	·············	¼杯
醬油	·············	⅓杯
┌ 冰糖	·············	½大匙
│ 酒	·············	1大匙
① 黑醋	·············	½小匙
└ 水	·············	1杯

1 整塊肉先以滾水川燙後取出，將表皮刮洗乾淨，切約2公分厚之片狀。
2 鍋燒熱，擺上肉片，加熱蒸發水份，並將肉煎香鏟至一邊。留油2大匙，炒香蒜頭，隨入醬油和肉稍炒拌，再加入①料煮滾，盛烤盅，蓋上鋁箔紙。
3 烤箱預熱至200℃(400°F)，烤盅置中層，烤約1－1½小時即可。

老師的叮嚀：

1 滷肉(焢肉)宜選帶有肥肉的較香Q。
2 喜歡稍焦香者，可於快烤好前掀開蓋子，以200℃(400°F)烤約10分鐘。
3 此道菜可配飯、麵，亦可夾麵包、荷葉包(或割包)食用。

2⅔ lb. (1200g) pork belly
¼ c. garlic, crushed
⅓ c. soy sauce

- ½ T. rock sugar
- ① 1T. wine
- ½ t. black vinegar
- 1c. water

1 Blanch pork in boiling water and remove. Rinse and scrape the skin; cut in 1" (2cm) thick slices.
2 Heat the pan and fry pork to extract moisture and until fragrant. Move pork to side of pan. In 2T. remaining oil, stir-fry garlic until fragrant. Add soy sauce and pork to stir-fry. Add ① and bring to boil; remove. Put in a baking casserole and seal with foil paper.
3 Preheat oven to 200°C (400°F). Bake pork in casserole on middle rack for 1 - 1½ hours until done; serve.

Footnotes:

1 Choose pork belly that contains fat to enhance flavor.
2 To enhance fragrance, remove foil before pork is done and roast at 200°C (400°F) for another 10 minutes.
3 This dish goes well with rice, noodles, bread, mandarin pancakes or Taiwanese steamed turnovers.

粉蒸肉
Spicy Steamed Pork

4人份／ **serves 4**

梅花肉（前腿肉）
.... 450公克（12兩）

① 醬油、酒 各2大匙
辣豆瓣醬、糖 各1小匙
薑、蒜末、蔥花 ... 各½大匙
水 3大匙

蒸肉粉（1包） .... ¼杯
荷葉 1葉
鋁箔紙（20公分×15公分） 4張

1 豬肉切成4大塊，加①料拌勻醃約30分鐘，再拌入蒸肉粉。荷葉以熱水泡軟洗淨，剪成4等份。

2 荷葉攤開，擺上肉塊，並淋醃汁包起，再以鋁紙包妥，依次包好成四份，置烤盅，上蓋備烤。

3 烤箱預熱至190°C（375°F），烤盅置中層，烤約1-1½小時即可。

老師的叮嚀：

1 粉蒸肉包荷葉有特殊的荷葉香，如無荷葉，直接以鋁紙包妥即可。

1lb. (450g) pork shoulder

① **2T. each: soy sauce, wine**
1t. each: hot bean paste, sugar
½ T. each (minced): ginger root, garlic, green onions
3T. water

¼ c. powder for steaming pork
1 lotus leaf
4 aluminum foil sheets, 8" × 6" (20cm × 15cm)

1 Chop pork into 4 pieces. Marinate in ① for about 30 minutes. Mix in powder for steaming pork. Rinse and soak lotus leaf in hot water until soft and clean; cut into 4 parts.

2 Place each pork piece on ¼ lotus leaf. Sprinkle on some marinade and fold closed; then wrap each in a foil sheet. Place on baking casserole and cover.

3 Preheat oven to 190°C (375°F). Bake pork on middle rack for 1 - 1½ hours until done; serve.

Footnote:

1 Lotus leaf has a unique perfume flavor that is infused into the meat. If not available, directly wrap pork in foil paper.

高升排骨
Flavored Spareribs

4人份／serves 4

小排骨 ········ 600公克(1斤)

① 酒 ················ 1大匙
白醋 ··············· 2大匙
糖 ················ 3大匙
醬油 ··············· 4大匙
水 ················ 5大匙

1 小排骨切3公分長段,加①料,裝入烤盅,先煮開後加蓋或以鋁紙蓋妥。
2 烤箱預熱至200℃(400°F),烤盅置中層,烤約1小時即可。

老師的叮嚀:

1 燒排骨極普遍又好吃,但改用爛烤的方式就可省去長時間照顧的麻煩。
2 排骨加上糖、醋去燒烤,色澤及味道特別香美。
3 喜有酥香之外層,可於烤熟後打開鋁紙,再烤15分鐘即可。

1⅓ lb. (600g) spareribs

① 1T. wine
2T. vinegar
3T. sugar
4T. soy sauce
5T. water

1 Chop spareribs into 1¼" (3cm) pieces. Add ① and put in baking casserole. Bring to boil then cover or seal with foil paper.
2 Preheat oven to 200°C (400°F). Place casserole on middle rack and bake for 1 hour until done; serve.

Footnotes:

1 This is a popular dish. By baking rather than simmering, it requires less work and is therefore easy to prepare.
2 Baking spareribs with sugar and vinegar will enhance flavor and color.
3 For crisp surface, you may open the lid or foil paper after spareribs are done and roast for another 15 minutes.

香醋牛小排
Roast Beef Short Ribs and Vinegar

2人份／**serves 2**

帶骨牛小排4片
.... 450公克(12兩)

① ┌ 鹽 .... ½小匙
 └ 胡椒 .... ¼小匙

沙拉油 1大匙
蒜末 .... ½大匙

② ┌ 黑醋 1小匙
 │ 醬油 1大匙
 │ 糖 .... ½小匙
 └ 芫荽莖(切碎) 1小匙

1　牛小排可先將筋稍切開(以防收縮)再撒上①料。

2　烤箱預熱至220℃(425℉),將牛小排置抹油的烤架上,置上層,烤約10分鐘即可取出盛盤。

3　油1大匙燒熱,炒香蒜末,隨入②料煮滾,淋於烤好的牛小排上即可。

老師的叮嚀:

1　可依個人喜好之熟度,增減烤的時間。

2　亦可稍煎上色再入烤箱烤。

---

4 pieces of beef short ribs, 1lb. (450g)

① ┌ **½ t. salt**
 └ **¼ t. pepper**

1T. oil
½ T. minced garlic

② ┌ **1t. black vinegar**
 │ **1T. soy sauce**
 │ **½ t. sugar**
 └ **1t. minced coriander stems**

1　Lightly cut the rib's sinew to prevent contraction. Sprinkle with ①.

2　Preheat oven to 220°C (425°F). Roast ribs on greased upper rack for 10 minutes until done; remove and arrange on a plate.

3　Heat 1T. oil and stir-fry minced garlic. Add ② and bring to boil; remove. Pour over roasted ribs and serve.

Footnotes:

1　The roasting time may be changed according to desired doneness.

2　You may also fry ribs until light brown before roasting.

51

烤羊排
Roast Lamb Chops

羊排4片 … 約300公克（8兩）

① ┌ 鹽 ………………………… ½小匙
  └ 胡椒 …………………………… 適量

蛋（打散）………………… 1個
麵包粉 ………………………… ½杯
麵粉 …………………………… ¼杯

1 羊排以搥肉器稍搥鬆，撒上 ① 料，依序沾上麵粉、蛋液及麵包粉。

2 油2大匙燒至八分熱，入羊排兩面稍煎至金黃色。

3 烤箱預熱至190℃（375°F），羊排放在烤盤上，置中層，烤約5－10分鐘，至所需熟度即可。

老師的叮嚀：

1 羊排裹敷麵包粉後，常用炸的方式烹調，但較油膩，改用稍煎上色的方式再烤熟，可減少油的使用。

2 進口羊排肉質非常嫩，這種做法，非常好吃，不妨試試。

4 lamb chops, ⅔ lb. (300g)

① ┌ **½ t. salt**
  └ **pepper as desired**

1 beaten egg
½ c. bread crumbs
¼ c. flour

1 Tenderize lamb with a meat mallet then mix with ①. Dip in flour, beaten egg, and bread crumbs in that order.

2 Heat 2T. oil and fry lamb until a golden brown surface appears.

3 Preheat oven to 190°C (375°F). Place lamb on baking tray and roast on middle rack for 5 - 10 minutes until done; serve.

Footnote:

1 After dipped in bread crumbs, the lamb chop is usually deep-fried until done; yet, it is oily. Here it is fried to achieve a golden brown hue then roasted until done. The amount of oil is reduced.

一品牛小排
Royal Beef Short Ribs

牛小排2塊… 900公克(1½斤)

① ┌ 紅酒或酒················· 1½杯
　　 醬油 ·················· ½杯
　　 五香粉、鹽 ········ 各1小匙
　　 糖 ·················· ½大匙
　　 蒜頭(稍拍) ············· 5瓣
　　 芹菜、蒜苗 共150公克(4兩)
　　 (切段稍拍)
　　└ 水 ·················· 1½杯

鋁箔紙(30公分×30公分) 2張

② ┌ 檸檬片 ················· 3片
　　 檸檬汁 ················· 5大匙
　　 糖 ·················· 3大匙
　　 醋 ·················· 2大匙
　　 鹽 ·················· ¼小匙
　　└ 水 ·················· 3大匙

蒜頭(去皮切片) ········ 5瓣

1 牛小排以 ① 料浸泡一天以上，取出分別以鋁箔紙包妥。

2 烤箱預熱至180℃(350℉)，牛小排放烤架上置中層烤約1-1½小時，打開鋁箔紙續烤約15分鐘至稍呈焦色即可。

3 ②料煮開為檸檬糖醋醬。

4 食時可沾醬或與蒜片共食，更美味。

老師的叮嚀：

1 這種小排是牛肉上品，富彈性又有咀嚼感，非常美味，可在肉品專賣店買到。

2 醃泡之香料亦可隨喜好加百里香、玉桂葉或肉桂等，酒和水的比例亦可隨喜好增減。

---

2 lbs. (900g) beef short ribs

① ┌ 1½ c. red wine or wine
　　 ½ c. soy sauce
　　 1t. each: five-spice powder, salt
　　 ½ T. sugar
　　 5 garlic cloves, crushed
　　 total of ⅓ lb. (150g) (cut in sections and crushed): celery, fresh garlic spear
　　└ 1½ c. water

2 aluminum foil sheets, 12" × 12" (30cm × 30cm)

② ┌ 3 lemon slices
　　 5T. lemon juice
　　 3T. sugar
　　 2T. vinegar
　　 ¼ t. salt
　　└ 3T. water

5 garlic cloves, peeled and sliced

1 Marinate ribs in ① for at least 1 day; remove. Wrap ribs separately in each foil sheet.

2 Preheat oven to 180°C (350°F). Bake ribs on middle rack for 1 - 1½ hours. Open foil paper and roast for another 15 minutes until lightly scorched; remove.

3 Bring ② to boil and make sweet and sour lemon sauce.

4 Serve with sweet and sour lemon sauce or sliced garlic.

Footnote:

1 Spices such as cinnamon may be added in ingredient ① to enhance flavor. The amount of wine and water may also be changed according to personal preference.

桔汁牛肋條
Beef Ribs in Orange Juice

2人份／serves 2

牛肋條	…………………	6條
┌柳橙汁	…………………	3大匙
│番茄醬	…………………	5大匙
│白醋	…………………	½大匙
①│蜂蜜	…………………	1小匙
│黑醋	…………………	1小匙
│蒜末	…………………	1大匙
│洋蔥末	…………………	2大匙
└鹽、胡椒	…………………	適量

1 牛肋條浸泡在拌勻的 ① 料中醃3小時以上或隔夜。
2 烤箱預熱至220℃(425°F)，牛肋條放在抹油的烤架上，置中層，烤約10－15分鐘即可。

老師的叮嚀：

1 宜選美國牛肋條肉較嫩，亦可改用肩胛里肌替代。
2 ① 料之醃汁，可隨喜好增減。
3 亦可依喜好沾芥末醬食之。

6 beef rib fingers (10" long strips)

┌**3T. orange juice**
│**5T. ketchup**
│**½ T. vinegar**
│**1t. honey**
①│**1t. black vinegar**
│**1T. minced garlic**
│**2T. minced onions**
└**salt and pepper as desired**

1 Marinate beef in mixture ① for at least 3 hours or overnight.
2 Preheat oven to 220°C (425°F) and roast beef on greased middle rack of oven for about 10-15 minutes; serve.

Footnotes:

1 Choose tender beef rib fingers or replace with tenderloin.
2 Amount of marinade in ingredient ① may be changed to personal preference.
3 May be served with mustard sauce to individual taste.

沙茶牛肉
Beef and Barbecue Sauce

4人份／serves 4

腓力或沙朗牛排肉
·············· 450公克 (12兩)

① ┌ 沙茶醬 ·············· 4大匙
  │ 醬油 ·············· ½大匙
  │ 糖 ·············· 1小匙
  │ 太白粉 ·············· ½小匙
  └ 水 ·············· 3大匙

② ┌ 蔥末 ·············· 2大匙
  │ 薑末 ·············· ½大匙
  └ 蒜末 ·············· 1大匙

1 牛肉切2公分方塊備用。
2 將牛肉置於烤盅，淋上拌勻的 ①、② 料，上蓋或以鋁紙封妥。
3 烤箱預熱至200℃ (400°F)，烤盅置中層，烤約20～25分鐘即可

老師的叮嚀：
1 牛肉宜選美國牛肉，肉質較嫩。
2 ②料亦可先炒香，再拌入牛肉中。
3 這道菜牛肉滑嫩，湯汁可淋飯，如再加上青菜或湯即為一道簡餐。
4 若無烤盅，亦可以鋁箔紙包成四份烤，則烤的時間可以縮短，且一人食用一份，非常方便。
5 喜歡吃較生的肉時，烤的時間可再縮短，但牛肉一定要新鮮。

1lb. (450g) filet mignon or sirloin steak

① ┌ 4T. barbecue (Sa Tsa) sauce
  │ ½ T. soy sauce
  │ 1t. sugar
  │ ½ t. cornstarch
  └ 3T. water

② ┌ 2T. minced green onions
  │ ½ T. minced ginger root
  └ 1T. minced garlic

1 Cut steak into ¾" (2cm) cubes.
2 Put beef in a baking casserole and pour over mixtures ① and ②. Cover or seal with foil paper.
3 Preheat oven to 200°C (400°F). Bake beef on middle rack for 20-25 minutes; serve.

Footnotes:
1 You may stir-fry ② until fragrant then add in beef.
2 This dish goes well with rice. If also served with vegetables or soup, it becomes a one-dish-meal.
3 If baking casserole is not available, divide beef in four parts and wrap each part in foil paper. The baking time will be reduced by 30 minutes.
4 The baking time for beef may be changed according to desired tenderness.

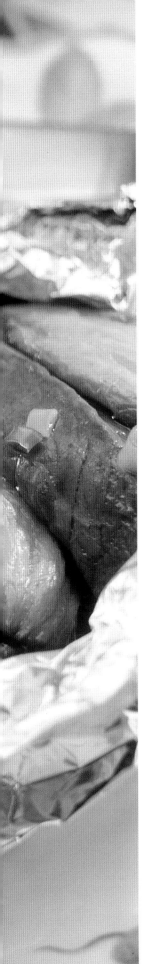

紙包芒果牛柳
Beef and Mango

腓力牛排 … 450公克（12兩）

①
- 蠔油、酒 ………… 各1大匙
- 麻油 ………………… 1小匙
- 糖 ………………… ½小匙
- 鹽 ………………… ¼小匙
- 胡椒 ………………… 適量
- 玉米粉（或太白粉）… 2小匙

芒果 ………………… 2個

②
- 蔥花 ………………… 1大匙
- 薑末 ………………… 1小匙

鋁箔紙(50公分×50公分) 2張
奶油 ………………… 適量

1 牛肉切成4片，加①料調味，芒果去皮取肉共4片。

2 鋁紙中間塗少許奶油，再以一片牛肉一片芒果的順序擺好，撒上②料，包成長方型。

3 烤箱預熱至200℃（400°F），牛肉置中層，烤約25-35分鐘至所需之熟度即可。

老師的叮嚀：

1 亦可分開包成4份入烤箱，則烤的時間可縮短，且分食較方便。

2 牛肉融入芒果的味道特別香醇，若無芒果，亦可以罐頭水蜜桃替代。

1lb. (450g) filet mignon steak

①
- 1T. each: oyster oil, wine
- 1t. sesame oil
- ½ t. sugar
- ¼ t. salt
- pepper as desired
- 2t. cornstarch

2 mangoes

②
- 1T. minced green onion
- 1t. minced ginger root

2 aluminum foil sheets, 20" × 20" (50cm × 50cm)
butter as desired

1 Cut steak into 4 slices; marinate in ①. Peel and seed mangoes; cut into 4 pieces.

2 Brush some oil on middle part of the foil paper. Place on a slice of beef and mango alternately; sprinkle with ②. Wrap in two layers of foil paper to form a rectangular shape.

3 Preheat oven to 200°C (400°F). Bake beef on middle rack for 25-35 minutes until done; serve.

Footnotes:

1 By wrapping a beef and a mango piece in individual foil sheets, the baking time will be reduced and it is easy to serve.

2 If mangoes are not available, replace them with canned peaches.

烤牛肉
Baked Steak

沙朗或腓力牛排 1 塊
　　………… 900 公克 (1½ 斤)

① ┌ 醬油　　………… 6 大匙
　　│ 糖　　　………… 2 大匙
　　│ 酒　　　………… 2 大匙
　　│ 蒜末　　………… 1 大匙
　　└ 胡椒粒　………… 1 小匙

　　鋁箔紙 (50 公分×50 公分)　2 張

1　牛肉以 ① 料醃 3 小時以上，取出，將肥肉面朝上，以鋁箔紙包妥。

2　烤箱預熱至 180°C (350°F)，牛肉置中層，烤約 40 分鐘後打開鋁紙，再續烤約 15 分鐘至表面略呈焦狀即可。

老師的叮嚀：

1　此菜以整塊牛肉烤出後，切片分食當主菜，份量可隨人數增減，非常方便。

2　烤牛肉所需時間，可依個人喜好熟度增減。

3　① 料可以醬油¼杯、酒 2 大匙、辣醬油 1 大匙、鹽½小匙替代，亦可僅抹上胡椒、鹽等去烤，以保持肉的原味及鮮嫩。

4　烤好後之肉汁可加些香料、調味料做成調味醬汁，為簡化過程，直接當調味汁亦非常美味。

1 sirloin or filet mignon steak, 2lb. (900g)

① ┌ **6T. soy sauce**
　　│ **2T. sugar**
　　│ **2T. wine**
　　│ **1T. minced garlic**
　　└ **1t. pepper corns**

2 aluminum foil sheets, 20" × 20" (50cm × 50cm)

1　Marinate steak in ① for at least 3 hours; remove. Wrap steak, fat side up, in foil paper.

2　Preheat oven to 180°C (350°F). Bake steak on middle rack for about 40 minutes. Open foil paper and bake for another 15 minutes until steak becomes a little singed on the surface; serve.

Footnotes:

1　Slice steak according to number of guests and serve as a main course.

2　Adjust baking time to get desired tenderness for personal preference.

3　Ingredients in ① may be replaced by ¼ c. soy sauce, 2T. wine, 1T. spicy soy sauce, and ½T. salt. Or directly rub pepper and salt on steak, then bake to ensure tenderness and original flavor.

4　Add spices to juice from the baked steak to make seasoning sauce.

拌青菜
Boiled Vegetables

豆芽菜 ········ 225公克(6兩)

① ┌ 麻油 ············ 1小匙－1大匙
   │ 芝麻(炒香壓碎) ····· 1小匙
   └ 鹽··· ½小匙，胡椒 ··· 適量

菠菜(或茼蒿菜) 300公克(8兩)

② ┌ 醬油 ··················· 1大匙
   │ 芝麻(炒香壓碎) ····· 2小匙
   │ 麻油 ··················· 1小匙
   └ 胡椒、鹽 ········· 各¼小匙

1 豆芽菜、菠菜洗淨，菠菜切段，分別以滾水燙熟速撈出，擠去水份，分別再拌入 ① 、 ② 料即可。

½ lb. (225g) bean sprouts

① ┌ **1t. - 1T. sesame oil**
   │ **1t. fried and ground sesame seeds**
   │ **½ t. salt**
   └ **pepper as desired**

⅔ lb. (300g) spinach or garland chrysanthemum

② ┌ **1T. soy sauce**
   │ **2t. fried and ground sesame seeds**
   │ **1t. sesame oil**
   └ **¼ t. each: pepper, salt**

1 Rinse bean sprouts and spinach. Cut spinach into sections. Blanch separately in boiling water until done; remove immediately. Squeeze juice off. Mix separately with ① and ②; serve.

韓式烤肉
Korean Barbecued Meat

肋眼牛肉、豬肉或雞肉
········· 450公克(12兩)

醬油 ··················· 4大匙

① ┌ 糖 ··················· 3大匙
   │ 酒、蘋果擠汁 ····· 各1大匙
   │ 芝麻(炒香磨碎) ····· 1大匙
   │ 蒜末 ··· 2小匙 ，胡椒··· 適量
   └ 苜蓿芽 ············ 150公克(4兩)

生菜葉 ··················· 12片

1 肉切約0.5公分薄片(或買現成烤肉片)，烤前拌入 ① 料。
2 烤箱預熱至220℃(425°F)，肉片排在抹油的烤架上，置中層，烤約5分鐘即可，可以苜蓿芽、生菜葉包捲而食。

老師的叮嚀：
1 用鐵板邊煎邊食亦很有味道。
2 此道菜味道濃，以米飯或涼拌青菜配食，就是營養的一餐。

1lb. (450g) rib eye beef, pork, or chicken

4T. soy sauce

① ┌ **3T. sugar**
   │ **1T. each: wine, squeezed apple juice**
   │ **1T. fried and ground sesame seeds**
   │ **2t. minced garlic pepper as desired**
   └ **⅓ lb. (150g) baby clover**

12 lettuce leaves

1 Cut meat into ¼" (0.5cm) thick slices or buy meat slices for barbecuing. Mix meat with ① before roasting.
2 Preheat oven to 220°C (425°F). Arrange meat on greased middle rack and roast for 5 minutes until done; remove. Roll meat and baby clover in lettuce leaves and serve.

Footnotes:
1 Frying meat in iron plate is another choice.
2 This dish is salty, so it goes well with rice or boiled vegetables.

中式牛排
Garlic Flavored Steak

牛排肉2片 ⋯ 約300公克(8兩)

① ┌ 鹽 ⋯⋯⋯⋯⋯⋯⋯ ¼小匙
　 └ 胡椒 ⋯⋯⋯⋯⋯⋯ 適量

蒜末 ⋯⋯⋯⋯⋯⋯ 1小匙

② ┌ 酒 ⋯⋯⋯⋯⋯⋯ 1-2大匙
　 │ 醬油 ⋯⋯⋯⋯⋯⋯ 2小匙
　 └ 糖 ⋯⋯⋯⋯⋯⋯ ½小匙

洋菇(切片) ┐
青紅椒(切片) ┘ ⋯⋯⋯⋯ 1杯

1　將有烙條之鐵板燒熱並抹少許油，牛排撒上①料，在鐵板上烙出菱形烤紋後置烤盤上。

2　烤箱預熱至200℃(400°F)，牛肉置中層，烤約10分鐘，至喜好之熟度即可取出裝盤，並以炒熟洋菇及青紅椒置旁配食。

3　油1小匙燒熱，以小火炒香蒜末，入②料煮滾成調味汁，淋於烤好的牛肉上即可。

老師的叮嚀：

1　烙紋之方法：以有烙條的鐵板燒熱，抹上油，牛肉以30度對著左上角之方向擺上，烙成斜紋，同面再以30度對著右上角之方向擺上，烙至菱形紋形成即成（各烙約30秒即可）。

2　使用烙條之鐵板煎出之牛排較美觀，若無，可以平底鍋略煎後再烤。

3　牛排淋上中式調味汁，非常美味，亦可以現成的黑胡椒醬、磨菇醬配食。

2 steaks, ⅔ lb. (300g)

① ┌ ¼ t. salt
　 └ pepper as desired

1t. minced garlic

② ┌ 1 - 2T. wine
　 │ 2t. soy sauce
　 └ ½ t. sugar

total of 1c. (sliced) :
button mushrooms,
green peppers, red
peppers

1　Heat grill and brush on some oil. Sprinkle ① on steaks and fry until rhombic lines form on the surface; remove. Place on a baking tray.

2　Preheat oven to 200°C (400°F). Roast steaks on middle rack for 10 minutes until desired tenderness; remove. Place on a plate and garnish with cooked mushrooms and peppers.

3　Heat 1t. oil and stir-fry minced garlic over low heat until fragrant. Add ② and bring to a boil to become a seasoning sauce; remove. Pour over steaks and serve.

Footnotes:

1　Method for making rhombic lines on steak surface: Heat grill and brush on some oil. Fry steaks by putting obliquely by 30° angle to the left then to the right pointed end to form rhombic lines. (Fry each side for 30 seconds.)

2　If grill is not available, fry steaks in pan before roasting.

3　Black pepper sauce or mushroom sauce may replace seasoning sauce.

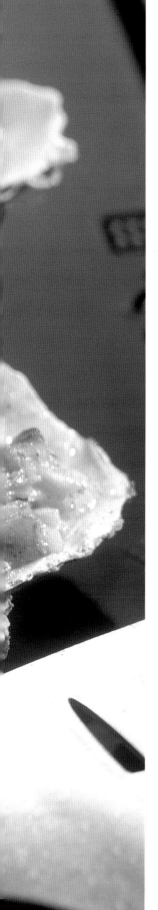

香烤生蠔
Baked Oysters

帶殼生蠔	…………	8個
芋頭(切小丁)	………	½杯
① 洋蔥末	……………	3大匙
蒜末	……………	1小匙
薑末	……………	1小匙
蔥末	……………	1大匙
② 美乃滋	……………	3大匙
奶油	……………	1大匙
胡椒	……………	適量
鹽	……………	適量
炸油	……………	2杯

1 生蠔肉挖出，洗淨瀝乾，再放回原殼上。

2 炸油燒熱，先將芋頭丁炸微黃，再入①料炸30秒，一同撈出，待涼，拌入②料，抹於生蠔上。

3 烤箱預熱至200℃(400°F)，生蠔放在烤盤上，置中層，烤約10分鐘，再以上火續烤約5分鐘至呈金黃色即可。

老師的叮嚀：

1 生蠔可在大的海鮮店買到，亦可以淡菜替代。

2 為求簡化亦可將生蠔直接抹上②料烤熟，也同樣好吃。

---

8 oysters in shell
½ c. taro, chopped in cubes

① **3T. minced onions**
1t. each (minced) : garlic, ginger root
1T. minced green onions

② **3T. mayonnaise**
1T. butter
pepper as desired
salt as desired

2c. oil for deep-frying

1 Take meat out of shells. Wash and drain dry; return meat to the shells.

2 Heat oil and deep-fry taro until light brown. Add ① and deep-fry for another 30 seconds; remove. When cool, mix with ② and rub on oysters.

3 Preheat oven to 200°C (400°F). Arrange oysters on the tray and bake on middle rack of oven for 10 minutes. Turn to upper heater or move the tray to upper rack; bake for another 5 minutes until golden brown; serve.

Footnotes:

1 Mussels may be substituted for oysters.

2 For simplification, directly spread mixture ② on oysters then bake to achieve the same delicious taste.

蘆筍鮭魚捲
Salmon Rolls and Asparagus

4人份／serves 4

鮭魚肉 …… 450公克(12兩)
蘆筍(12公分長) ……… 8支

①
- 酒 ………………… 1大匙
- 鹽 ………………… 1小匙
- 胡椒 ……………… 適量
- 太白粉 …………… 1大匙

1 鮭魚以一刀不斷一刀切斷之連刀法切成四大片，拌入 ① 料，蘆筍以滾水川燙2分鐘後取出。

2 魚片攤開，擺上 2 支蘆筍，捲起成圓柱形共4捲，封口向下置烤盤上。

3 烤箱預熱至220℃ (425℉)，魚置中層，烤約20分鐘至熟即可。

老師的叮嚀：

1 鮭魚亦可以醃燻鮭魚或其他魚肉取代。

2 為求色澤更美，亦可先煎呈金黃色再入烤箱烤。

1lb. (450g) fresh salmon
8 asparagus spears,
   5" (12cm) long

①
- **1T. wine**
- **1t. salt**
- **pepper as desired**
- **1T. cornstarch**

1 Make slashes on salmon and cut all the way through only on alternate cuts to make 4 slices; marinate in ①. Blanch asparagus in hot water for 2 minutes; remove.

2 Put 2 asparagus spears on each salmon slice and roll to form a cylinder. Place rolls on the baking tray with sealed side down.

3 Preheat oven to 220°C (425°F). Bake rolls on middle rack for 20 minutes until done; serve.

Footnotes:

1 Smoked salmon or other fish may be substituted for fresh salmon.

2 Fry salmon rolls before baking in order to achieve a golden brown hue.

鹽焗蝦
Salty Shrimp

鮮蝦 ………… 300公克(8兩)

① ⎡ 酒 ………………… 1大匙
   | 鹽 ………………… 1小匙
   | 薑片 ……………… 2片
   | 蒜末 ……………… 1小匙
   ⎣ 胡椒 ……………… 適量

鋁箔紙(50公分×50公分) 2張

1 蝦剪除蝦鬚，抽去腸泥洗淨瀝乾，加①料拌勻，以鋁紙包妥。

2 烤箱預熱至220℃(425°F)，蝦置中層，烤約15分鐘即可。

老師的叮嚀：

1 蝦不宜烤太久，剛熟最有彈性，否則會乾澀不好吃。

2 可隨喜好將蒜末改成檸檬汁1大匙，亦有特殊風味。

⅔ lb. (300g) shrimp

① ⎡ **1T. wine**
   | **1t. salt**
   | **2 slices of ginger root**
   | **1t. minced garlic**
   ⎣ **pepper as desired**

**2 aluminum foil sheets,
20" × 20" (50cm × 50cm)**

1 Cut off antennae from shrimp and devein; rinse and drain. Add ① and mix thoroughly. Wrap shrimp in foil paper.

2 Preheat oven to 220°C (425°F). Bake shrimp on middle rack for 15 minutes and serve.

Footnotes:

1 Shrimp should be baked until done then removed immediately to achieve best taste. If overcooked, they become dry and hard.

2 1T. lemon juice may be substituted for minced garlic in ingredient ① to change flavor according to personal preference.

日式鮭魚頭
Baked Salmon Head

2人份／serves 2

鮭魚頭 ½個 … 450公克(12兩)

① ┌ 酒 ………………… 1大匙
　 │ 味醂(圖1) …………… 1大匙
　 │ 柴魚醬油(圖2) ……… 3大匙
　 │ 鹽 ………………… ¼小匙
　 │ 蔥 ………………… 2支
　 └ 薑 ………………… 2片

（圖1）　　　　　（圖2）

1 鮭魚頭洗淨，拭乾水份，以①料醃約1小時。

2 烤箱預熱至190℃（375°F），鮭魚放在抹油的烤架上，置中層烤約20－25分鐘即可。

■ 味醂：用糯米釀製而成，色透明味甜之液體，為日本料理常用之調味料。

■ 柴魚醬油：是由醬油及柴魚片、魚干、海帶（昆布）、海貝等原料及調味料製成，為日本常用之調味料，可做沾醬、醃料，並可放於涼麵、湯麵及蒸蛋中。

老師的叮嚀：

1 鮭魚是深海魚，為優良魚類，肉可做生魚片或各式料理。

2 魚頭通常拿來煮湯，但改以烤的方式亦非常美味可口，目前超市很容易購買，不妨試試。

3 如使用整個魚頭，宜剖開成二半，較易烤熟。

½ salmon head, 1lb. (450g)

① ┌ 1T. wine
　 │ 1T. mirin (Fig.1)
　 │ 3T. tzuyou (Fig.2)
　 │ ¼ t. salt
　 │ 2 green onions
　 └ 2 slices of ginger root

1 Clean fish head and pat dry. Marinate in ① for about 1 hour.

2 Preheat oven to 190°C (375°F). Bake salmon on greased middle rack for 20 - 25 minutes until done; serve.

■ Mirin: A transparent, sweet cooking wine made from glutinous rice, frequently used in Japanese cooking.

■ Tzuyou: Made of soy sauce, bonito shavings, small dried fish, dried seaweed, and sea mussels; frequently used in Japanese cooking. It is used as dipping sauce, marinade, or added in noodles and steamed eggs.

Footnotes:

1 Salmon live most of their lives in deep waters and therefore are a healthier variety of fish. Clean fish are suitable for sashimi.

2 Salmon head is usually cooked for soup. Yet, baked is also delicious.

3 If a whole fish head is used, cut in half to cook thoroughly.

烤龍蝦
Baked Lobster

龍蝦1隻 … 約450公克 (12兩)

① ┌ 鹽 ………………………… ¼小匙
　 └ 胡椒 ……………………… 適量

② ┌ 奶油 ……………………… 2小匙
　 └ 蒜末 ……………………… 1小匙

1 龍蝦對剖成二半，處理乾淨拭乾水份，撒上 ① 料並抹上 ② 料，置烤盤上。

2 烤箱預熱至230℃ (450°F)，龍蝦置中層烤約15分鐘至熟即可。

老師的叮嚀：

1 龍蝦宜買活的，較鮮美，烤至肉剛熟即應取出，以保持蝦肉的彈性。

2 若無龍蝦亦可以明蝦取代。

1 lobster, 1lb. (450g)

① ┌ **¼ t. salt**
　 └ **pepper as desired**

② ┌ **2t. butter**
　 └ **1t. minced garlic**

1 Cut lobster in half; clean and pat dry. Sprinkle with ① and ② then place on baking tray.

2 Preheat oven to 230°C (450°F). Bake lobster on middle rack for about 15 minutes until done; serve.

Footnotes:

1 Choose live lobster and remove from oven immediately when it is done to ensure flavor and texture.

2 If lobster is not available, large prawns may be used.

蒜香烤魚
Baked Fish and Garlic

鱒魚1條　……450公克(12兩)

① ┌ 奶油　………………… 2大匙
　 │ 蒜末　………………… 2大匙
　 │ 鹽　…………… ½－1小匙
　 │ 胡椒　………………… ¼小匙
　 └ 芫荽莖　……………… 1大匙

鋁箔紙(50公分×50公分)　1張

1　鱒魚處理乾淨，拭乾水份，鋁箔紙中間抹油備用。

2　魚擺上 ① 料，以鋁箔紙包妥。

3　烤箱預熱至200℃(400°F)，魚放在烤架上，置中層，烤約30分鐘即可。

老師的叮嚀：

1　鱒魚亦可改用各種較無腥味之鮮魚，如石斑魚、鮭魚或螃蟹等。

---

1 trout, 1 lb. (450g)

① ┌ **2T. butter**
　 │ **2T. minced garlic**
　 │ **½ - 1 t. salt**
　 │ **¼ t. pepper**
　 └ **1T. coriander stems**

**1 aluminum foil sheet,
　　20" × 20" (50cm × 50cm)**

1　Rinse trout and pat dry. Brush oil on middle part of foil paper; set aside.

2　Sprinkle ① on trout and wrap with foil paper.

3　Preheat oven to 200°C (400°F). Bake trout on middle rack for 30 minutes until done; serve.

Footnote:

1　Fresh fish such as grouper, salmon, or crab may be substituted for trout.

奶油螃蟹
Crab and Butter

2人份／**serves 2**

螃蟹1隻‥‥‥ 450公克（12兩）
①
　奶油　‥‥‥‥‥‥‥ 2大匙
　蒜末　‥‥‥‥‥‥‥ 1大匙
　胡椒、鹽 ‥‥‥‥‥‥ 適量
　嫩薑末 ‥‥‥‥‥‥ 1小匙
鋁箔紙（30公分×50公分） 2張

1　蟹剝殼，去鰓，洗淨，蟹身剁塊。

2　鋁紙攤開疊好，中間刷少許奶油，擺上蟹塊，拌入 ① 料，蓋上蟹蓋，將鋁紙包妥。

3　烤箱預熱至220℃（425°F），螃蟹置中層，烤約30-40分鐘即可。

老師的叮嚀：

1　螃蟹可用青蟹、花蟹、紅蟳蟹，但宜選活的，且肉質肥的較為鮮美。

2　烤完後的奶油蒜汁，可拌飯、麵線或煮粥，味道亦非常鮮美。

3　螃蟹宜用雙層鋁紙包妥，以防刺破湯汁流失。

1 crab, 1lb. (450g)
①
2T. butter
1T. minced garlic
pepper and salt as desired
1t. minced baby ginger
root
2 aluminum foil sheets,
12" × 20" (30cm × 50cm)

1　Remove shell and gills of crab. Rinse and chop into pieces.

2　Spread foil paper and brush some oil on middle part. Put on crab pieces and mix with ①. Cover with crab shell then wrap in foil paper.

3　Preheat oven to 220°C (425°F). Bake crab on middle rack of oven for 30 - 40 minutes; serve.

Footnotes:

1　The garlic butter sauce after baking is tasty and it goes well with rice, noodles, or if used for cooking congee.

2　Wrap crab in double layers of foil paper to avoid loss of juices in case foil is pierced by crab claws or shell.

焗珍味鮑魚
Baked Abalone

熟鮑魚（切2公分方塊）…12塊
① ⎡醬油膏 ………………………2小匙
　 ⎣蒜泥 ……………………………1小匙
美乃滋 …………………………3大匙
烤田螺容器

1 將鮑魚塊放入烤田螺容器凹洞中，各滴少許 ①
　料，再擠上適量的美乃滋。

2 烤箱預熱220°C（425°F），容器置中層，烤約10分
　鐘至呈金黃色即可。

老師的叮嚀：

1 烤田螺為法國名菜，改以鮑魚烹製，簡單又美味，
　很適合宴客。

2 鮑魚可使用罐頭或真空包裝之調味鮑魚，調味鮑魚
　汁可替代醬油膏。

**12 seasoned abalone, cut
in ¾" (2cm) cubes**

① ⎡**2t. thick soy sauce**
　 ⎣**1t. garlic paste**

**3T. mayonnaise
cookware for baking
conches**

1 Put abalone cubes in holes of baking cookware.
Sprinkle on each abalone a few drops of ① and
add mayonnaise as desired.

2 Preheat oven to 220°C (425°F). Bake abalone
in cookware on middle rack for 10 minutes until
golden brown; serve.

Footnotes:

1 Baked conches is a famous French dish. Baked
abalone is also easy to prepare and tasty. It is a
good dish for banquets.

2 Use canned or vacuum-packed seasoned
abalone. The seasoning sauce may be
substituted for thick soy sauce.

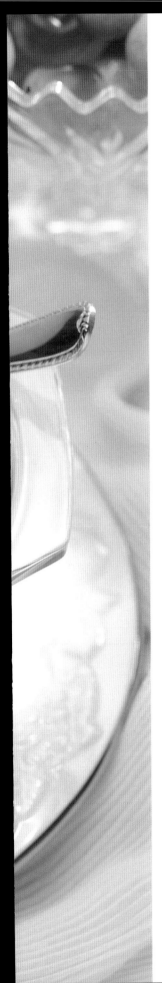

蒜香蛤蜊
Clams and Garlic

蛤蜊或海瓜子　600公克(1斤)
酒 ……………………1大匙
蒜末 ………………1-2大匙

1 蛤蜊排於寬淺之烤盅，加酒並撒上蒜末，加蓋或以鋁紙包妥。

2 烤箱預熱至200℃(400℉)，烤盅置中層，烤約15分鐘即可。

老師的叮嚀：

1 宜選擇透明的烤盅，見蛤蜊一開口，表示已熟，即可取出。

2 以烤架烤蛤蜊，需去韌帶，否則烤後蛤蜊張開，湯汁會流失。

3 為了省去韌帶的麻煩，可裝於烤盅，燜烤後湯汁才不會流失，且本身的鹹味剛好。

**1⅓ lb. (600g) clams or
  Manila clams
1T. wine
1 - 2T. minced garlic**

1 Arrange clams on a shallow baking casserole dish. Add wine and sprinkle with garlic. Cover or seal with foil paper.

2 Preheat oven to 200°C (400°F). Bake clams in casserole dish on middle rack for 15 minutes until done; serve.

Footnotes:

1 Choose a transparent casserole dish to check whether clams are done or not. When clams open up, they are done; remove at once.

2 If you bake clams directly on rack, cut sinew to prevent loss of juices as they open up.

焗海鮮
Seafood Gratin

┌─ 蛤蜊肉 ─┐
① 大蝦仁 ├ … 約300公克（8兩）
└─ 鮮干貝 ─┘
└ 洋菇 ……………………… 1杯

洋蔥 …………………… ½個
奶油 …………………… 3大匙
麵粉 …………………… 3大匙
奶水 …………………… 1¼杯

┌─ 酒 ……………………… 1大匙
② 鹽 ……………………… ½小匙
└─ 胡椒粉 ………………… 適量

┌─ 鮮奶油（或奶水）……… ¼杯
③ 鹽 ……………………… ½小匙
└─ 胡椒粉 ………………… 適量

乾酪絲（起司）………… ½杯

1 蝦仁去腸泥，洗淨拭乾。洋菇切片，洋蔥切丁。

2 油2大匙燒熱，將洋蔥炒香，隨入①料以大火炒1分鐘，加②料拌炒至湯汁收乾，裝入烤盅。

3 奶油3大匙，以小火加熱，先炒香麵粉至均勻，再徐徐倒入奶水，邊倒邊攪拌煮至濃稠狀，加入③料攪拌至滾，取出淋於海鮮上，撒上乾酪絲。

4 烤箱預熱至220℃（425°F），以上火烤約10分鐘即可。

老師的叮嚀：

1 海鮮可依喜好選用魚肉、墨魚等皆可，但一定要新鮮。

2 焗上色時，溫度需高些，且可只用上火。

3 此道菜可先做好，於食用前再入烤箱焗即可，宴客非常方便。

┌─ **total of ⅔ lb. (300g): clam meat, shelled large shrimp, scallops**
①
└─ **1c. button mushrooms**

½ onion
3T. butter
3T. flour
1¼ c. evaporated milk

┌─ **1T. wine**
② **½ t. salt**
└─ **pepper as desired**

┌─ **¼ c. cream or evaporated milk**
③ **½ t. salt**
└─ **pepper as desired**

½ c. shredded cheese

1 Devein shelled shrimp; rinse and drain. Slice mushrooms and chop onions.

2 Heat 2T. oil and stir-fry onion until fragrant; add ① and stir-fry over high heat for 1 minute. Add ② and stir-fry until almost dry. Pour mixture into a baking casserole.

3 Heat 3T. butter over low heat and stir into flour until fragrant and even. Add in evaporated milk gradually and stir occasionally until thick. Add ③ and stir until boiling; remove. Pour over seafood and sprinkle with cheese.

4 Preheat oven to 220°C (425°F). Bake seafood under upper heat for 10 minutes; serve.

Footnotes:

1 Fish, octopus, or any desired seafood may be used in ingredient ①.

2 Bake this dish on upper rack of oven or use upper heat for a golden brown surface.

3 For a banquet, prepare this dish in advance and bake before serving for a nice color.

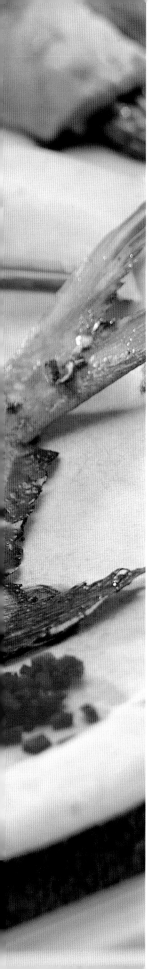

五香烤魚
Five-Spice Pomfret

2-4 人份／ serves 2-4

鯧魚1條…… 450公克(12兩)

① ┌ 酒 ………………………… 1大匙
  │ 五香粉、糖 ……… 各1小匙
  │ 鹽 ………………………… ½小匙
  └ 醬油、蒜末 ……… 各1大匙

1 魚洗淨拭乾,兩面劃刀痕,以①料醃泡30分鐘。
2 烤箱預熱至200℃(400°F),魚放在抹油的烤架上,置中層烤約30分鐘至熟即可。

老師的叮嚀:

1 魚劃上刀痕較易熟,也易入味,且烤至稍呈焦色時會更香。
2 鯧魚可改用其他新鮮較無腥味的魚,如:迦納、白帶魚等。
3 魚翅、魚尾等可沾上粗鹽,以防烤焦。

1 pomfret, 1lb. (450g)

① ┌ **1T. wine**
  │ **1t. each: five-spice**
  │   **powder, sugar**
  │ **½ t. salt**
  │ **1T. each: soy sauce,**
  └   **minced garlic**

1 Rinse pomfret and pat dry. Score the flesh on both sides and marinate in ① for 30 minutes.
2 Preheat oven to 200°C (400°F). Bake fish on greased middle rack for 30 minutes until done; serve.
3 Before baking, rub salt on fins to avoid scorching.

Footnotes:

1 Score the flesh on both sides so that it will absorb the sauce more easily and cook through quickly.
2 Fresh fish such as ghana or ribbonfish may replace pomfret.

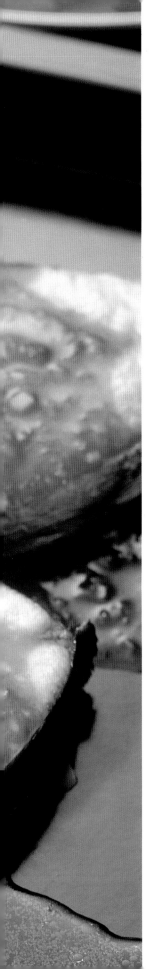

茄汁淋魚
Fish Covered with Ketchup

4 人份／serves 4

魚4片 ········ 450公克(12兩)

① ┌ 酒 ·························· 1大匙
　 └ 鹽 ·························· 1小匙

② ┌ 洋蔥(切碎) ·············· ½杯
　 │ 蒜末、薑末 ········ 各½大匙
　 └ 辣椒醬 ·················· 1小匙

③ ┌ 番茄醬 ·················· 3大匙
　 │ 鹽 ·························· ½小匙
　 │ 酒、糖 ············ 各½大匙
　 │ 麻油、太白粉 ····· 各1小匙
　 └ 高湯或水 ·············· ½杯

1 魚拭乾水份，拌入 ① 料醃約1小時。

2 烤箱預熱至220℃(425℉)，魚放在抹油的烤架上，置中層，烤約15分鐘至熟。

3 油3大匙燒熱，炒香 ② 料，加入 ③ 料煮成濃稠狀，淋於烤好之魚片上即成。

老師的叮嚀：

1 亦可用現成的乾燒醬淋上。

2 魚用烤的比用煎的少油煙，但有些魚肉油質較低，烤出之後稍乾，可淋上我們喜愛的調味汁，即非常好吃。

3 也可用整條魚來做，可在魚身上劃2－3刀，較易熟。

---

4 fish fillets, 1lb. (450g)

① ┌ 1T. wine
　 └ 1t. salt

② ┌ ½ c. minced onions
　 │ ½ T. each (minced): garlic, ginger root
　 └ 1t. chili sauce

③ ┌ 3T. ketchup
　 │ ½ t. salt
　 │ ½ T. each: wine, sugar
　 │ 1t. each: sesame oil, cornstarch
　 └ ½ c. stock or water

1 Pat fish dry and marinate in ① for 1 hour.

2 Preheat oven to 220°C (425°F). Grease middle rack of oven and bake fish for 15 minutes until done; remove.

3 Heat 3T. oil; stir-fry ② until fragrant. Add ③ and cook until liquid thickens. Pour over the baked fish and serve.

Footnotes:

1 Ready-made sauce may be used to pour over the baked fish in step 3.

2 Baking rather than frying fish will reduce oily smoke. Yet, lean fish may become dry from baking. Therefore, pour on seasoning sauce to enhance flavor and taste.

3 If whole fish is used, make 2 to 3 slashes on both surfaces of fish to enhance flavor and ensure it is thoroughly cooked.

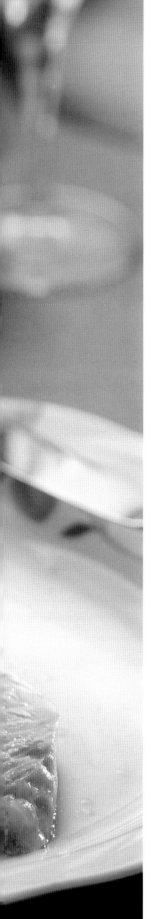

四蔬鮭魚
Salmon and Vegetables

鮭魚4片 ‧‧‧‧‧‧ 600公克(1斤)

① ┌ 鹽 ‧‧‧‧‧‧‧‧‧‧‧‧‧‧‧‧‧‧‧ 1小匙
　├ 胡椒 ‧‧‧‧‧‧‧‧‧‧‧‧‧‧‧‧‧ ¼小匙
　├ 酒 ‧‧‧‧‧‧‧‧‧‧‧‧‧‧‧‧‧‧‧ 1大匙
　└ 檸檬汁 ‧‧‧‧‧‧‧‧‧‧‧‧‧‧ 1大匙

鋁箔紙(30公分×30公分) 4張

② ┌ 洋蔥絲
　├ 胡蘿蔔絲
　├ 蒜苗絲 ‧‧‧ 75公克(2兩)
　└ 西洋芹菜絲

1 鋁箔紙中間塗少許油，擺上鮭魚片，先撒上 ① 料，再擺上②料，分別包妥。

2 烤箱預熱至190°C(375°F)，鮭魚放在烤架或烤盤上，置中層，烤約15－20分鐘即可。

老師的叮嚀：

1 這道菜我在宴客時很常用，準備方便，也頗受客人的喜愛。

2 可先包妥放冰箱中冷藏，上桌前再烤熟即可，趁熱食用。

3 ②料可隨喜好增減。

---

4 salmon slices,
　1⅓ lb. (600g)

① ┌ **1t. salt**
　├ **¼ t. pepper**
　├ **1T. wine**
　└ **1T. lemon juice**

4 aluminum foil sheets,
　12" × 12" (30cm × 30cm)

② ┌ **Total of 2½ oz. (75g)**
　│ **(shredded): onions,**
　│ **carrots, fresh garlic,**
　└ **celery**

1 Brush some oil on middle of each foil paper; put on a salmon slice. Sprinkle ① and ② in order; wrap each slice in foil paper and set aside.

2 Preheat oven to 190°C (375°F). Bake salmon on middle rack for 15 - 20 minutes until done; serve.

Footnotes:

1 This is a good dish for banquets. It is easy to prepare and tasty.

2 Salmon may be wrapped and refrigerated, then bake until done and serve hot.

3 Ingredients in ② may be changed according to personal preference.

五味淋魚
Spicy Fish

2 人份／ serves 2

鱈魚2片 … 約300公克(8兩)

① 酒 ……………………… 1大匙
　 鹽 ……………………… ¼小匙
　 胡椒 …………………… 適量

② 蔥、薑、蒜末 …… 各1大匙
　 紅椒片 ………………… 1小匙
　 醬油、黑醋 ……… 各1大匙
　 糖 ……………………… ½小匙

1　鱈魚撒上①料，②料拌勻成調味汁。

2　烤箱預熱220℃(450°F)，魚放在抹油的烤架上，置中層，烤約15分鐘至熟，淋上②料即可。

老師的叮嚀：

1　鱈魚可以各種魚片替代，亦可先煎上色再入烤箱烤熟。

---

2 codfish fillets,
　⅔ lb. (300g)

① 1T. wine
　¼ t. salt
　pepper as desired

② 1T. each (minced): green
　　onions, ginger root,
　　garlic
　1t. sliced red pepper
　1T. each: soy sauce, black
　　vinegar
　½ t. sugar

1　Sprinkle ① on cod. Mix ②.

2　Preheat oven to 220°C (450°F). Bake cod on greased middle rack of oven for 15 minutes until done; remove. Pour over ② and serve.

Footnote:

1　Any fish fillets may replace cod. In addition, fish may be fried before baking to achieve a golden brown hue.

乾酪焗芹菜
Baked Cheese Celery

4人份／**serves 4**

西洋芹菜（切10公分長）8段
·············· 225公克（6兩）

① ┌ 鮪魚罐頭（壓碎）1罐　100公克
　├ 洋蔥末 ··············· 2大匙
　├ 美乃滋 ··············· 1大匙
　└ 胡椒 ····················· 適量

乾酪粉 ············· 1-2大匙

1　芹菜洗淨去老筋，① 料拌勻成餡。
2　將餡料填於芹菜凹糟中，上撒乾酪粉。
3　烤箱預熱至220℃（425°F），芹菜放在烤盤上，置上層，烤約10分鐘即可。

老師的叮嚀：

1　芹菜宜選中段部分，凹糟較深易填餡料。
2　喜歡保有芹菜的脆度，可用220℃（425°F）上火，烤至乾酪粉稍呈金黃色即可。
3　乾酪粉亦可以乾酪絲取代.

½ lb. (225g) celery, cut
　into 8 sections, 4"
　(10cm) long

① ┌ 3½ oz. (100g) canned
　│ 　tuna, crushed
　├ 2T. minced onions
　├ 1T. mayonnaise
　└ pepper as desired

1 - 2T. cheese powder

1　Rinse celery and cut off old stems. Mix ①
　thoroughly to make filling.
2　Stuff filling in indented part of celery. Sprinkle
　with cheese powder.
3　Preheat oven to 220°C (425°F). Place celery on
　baking plate and bake on middle rack for 10
　minutes until done; serve.

Footnotes:

1　Use middle part of celery, for its indented part is
　deep and easy to stuff.
2　For crispness, bake over upper heat at 220°C
　(425°F) until cheese becomes golden brown.
3　Cheese shreds may also replace powder.

烤香菇
Baked Black Mushrooms

2-4 人份／serves 2-4

鮮香菇(大)8朵 225公克(6兩)
柴魚醬油 ··············· 2大匙
①┌美乃滋 ··············· 2大匙
　└蔥末 ··············· 1小匙

1　香菇洗淨去蒂，以柴魚醬油醃拌後，於背面抹上①料，排於烤盤上。
2　烤箱預熱至220℃(425℉)，烤盤置中層，烤約10分鐘即可。

老師的叮嚀：

1　香菇應速洗淨瀝乾水份，避免泡水太久而太濕。
2　鮮香菇味道鮮美，加美乃滋去烤，別有特殊風味。
3　①料可隨喜好增減。

**8 large fresh Chinese
black mushrooms,
½ lb. (225g)
2T. tzuyou**
①┌**2T. mayonnaise**
　└**1t. minced green onion**

1　Rinse mushrooms and discard the stems. Marinate in dashi and brush ① on the underside of mushrooms. Arrange on the baking tray.
2　Preheat oven to 220℃ (425℉). Bake mushrooms on middle rack for 10 minutes; serve.

Footnotes:

1　Rinse mushrooms and pat dry right away. Don't soak too long.
2　The amount of ingredients in ① may be changed according to personal preference.

檸汁鮮菇
Mushrooms in Lemon Juice

4人份／serves 4

新鮮洋菇 …	450公克(12兩)
①｛ 奶油 ……………………	2大匙
鹽 ……………………	½小匙
胡椒 ……………………	¼小匙
檸檬汁 ……………………	2大匙
鋁箔紙(50公分×50公分)	2張

1 新鮮洋菇去蒂,拌入 ① 料,以鋁箔紙包妥。

2 烤箱預熱至220℃(425°F),置中層,烤約20分鐘即可。

老師的叮嚀:

1 新鮮洋菇可以新鮮香菇代替。

2 洋菇味道清甜,但烹煮時易變黑,加些檸檬汁可減緩變色且可增加香味。

3 洋菇宜選底部未開,且大小均勻者為佳。

1lb. (450g) fresh button mushrooms

①｛ 2T. butter
½ t. salt
¼ t. pepper
2T. lemon juice

2 aluminum foil sheets, 20" × 20" (50cm × 50cm)

1 Remove stems from mushrooms and mix with ①. Wrap in foil paper.

2 Preheat oven to 220°C (425°F). Bake mushrooms on middle rack for 20 minutes until done; serve.

Footnotes:

1 Fresh Chinese black mushrooms may be substituted for fresh button mushrooms.

2 Button mushrooms taste sweet; yet they become dark when cooked. So add lemon juice to maintain color and enhance flavor.

3 Fresh mushrooms of equal size and not split around the stem should be used.

梅菜苦瓜

Bitter Melon and Dried Mustard Cabbage

苦瓜1條⋯⋯ 450公克（12兩）
梅乾菜 ⋯⋯⋯⋯ 75公克（2兩）
蒜末 ⋯⋯⋯⋯⋯⋯⋯ 1大匙

① ┌ 糖 ⋯⋯⋯⋯⋯⋯⋯⋯ 1大匙
　　胡椒粉 ⋯⋯⋯⋯⋯⋯ ¼小匙
　　高湯 ⋯⋯⋯⋯⋯⋯⋯ 1½杯
　　└ 味精 ⋯⋯⋯⋯⋯⋯⋯ 隨意

1 苦瓜對剖成兩半，挖除瓜瓤，水燒開煮約5分鐘，撈出置烤盅。

2 梅乾菜洗淨，切碎，先用3大匙油炒蒜末，再放入梅乾菜炒香，加入①料燒開，淋於苦瓜上，蓋鍋或以鋁箔紙封妥。

3 烤箱預熱至200℃（400°F），烤盅置中層，烤約1－1½小時即可。

老師的叮嚀：

1 苦瓜炸過再滷非常好吃，也是素食的一道佳餚。

2 用烤的方式做亦非常好吃，若喜歡吃熟透些的，可以延長烤的時間。

---

1 bitter melon, 1lb. (450g)
2½ oz. (75g) dried mustard cabbage (Mei Gan Tsai)
1T. minced garlic

① ┌ **1T. sugar**
　　¼ t. pepper
　　└ **1½ c. slock**

1 Cut bitter melon in half and remove seeds. Boil water and cook melon for 5 minutes; remove. Put in a baking casserole.

2 Rinse mustard cabbage and mince. Heat 3T. oil and stir-fry minced garlic. Add mustard cabbage and stir-fry until fragrant. Add ① and bring to boil; remove. Pour over bitter melon; cover or seal with foil paper.

3 Preheat oven to 200°C (400°F). Bake bitter melon on middle rack for 1 - 1½ hours; serve.

Footnotes:

1 Deep-frying bitter melon before simmering is also tasty. This is a good dish for vegetarians.

2 You may increase the baking time to cook bitter melon more thoroughly.

蛤蜊角瓜
Clams and Sponge Gourd

角瓜1條 …… 450公克（12兩）
蛤蜊 ………… 300公克（8兩）
薑 ……………………… 6片
①┌熱高湯 ………………… ½杯
 │鹽 …………………… ½小匙
 └味精 ………………………適量

1 蛤蜊泡鹽水（水3杯加鹽1小匙），吐沙後洗淨撈出。

2 角瓜去皮，切約1公分厚片，排入烤盅，上置蛤蜊及薑片，並淋入調勻的 ① 料，蓋鍋或以鋁紙蓋妥。

3 烤箱預熱至220℃（425℉），烤盅置中層，烤約25分鐘即可。

老師的叮嚀：

1 蛤蜊的鮮味，加上絲瓜的甜味，特別清爽好吃。

2 蛤蜊一定要確實吐沙，二個蛤蜊對敲時，有清脆聲響者，為活的。

3 亦可以雙層鋁箔紙包妥烤熟。

1 sponge gourd, 1lb. (450g)
⅔ lb. (300g) clams
6 ginger root slices
①┌ **½ c. hot stock**
 └ **½ t. salt**

1 Soak clams in salty water (add 1t. salt in 3c. water) until the sand is released; remove and rinse.

2 Peel sponge gourd and cut in ½" (1cm) thick slices. Arrange in a baking casserole. Put on clams and ginger root. Pour over mixed ①; cover or seal with foil paper.

3 Preheat oven to 220°C (425°F). Bake clams in casserole on middle rack for about 25 minutes; serve.

Footnotes:

1 Clams must release the sand thoroughly. Choose live clams that sound crisp when struck together.

2 If a baking casserole is not available, wrap clams in double layers of foil sheets and bake.

奶汁烤白菜
Cabbage Gratin

4 人份／serves 4

大白菜⋯⋯⋯⋯ 1200公克(2斤)
洋火腿(切片)⋯⋯⋯⋯⋯ 2片
或瘦肉(切片)⋯ 75公克(2兩)
①「鹽⋯ 1½小匙，味精⋯ 少許
　└高湯⋯⋯ 2杯，糖⋯⋯ 1小匙
奶油⋯ 5大匙，麵粉⋯ 5大匙
洋蔥(切碎)⋯⋯⋯⋯⋯⋯ ½杯
②「煮白菜湯汁⋯⋯⋯⋯⋯ 2½杯
　└濃縮奶水⋯⋯⋯⋯⋯⋯ ½杯

1　大白菜洗淨切粗塊，放入開水內川燙(由莖部先下)，略煮軟撈起。
2　油3大匙燒熱，先炒火腿，隨入白菜略炒，調 ① 料煮約5分鐘盛出，瀝乾湯汁(湯汁留用)，放入烤盅內。
3　奶油以小火燒熱，先把洋蔥炒軟，再放入麵粉炒香，並徐徐加入 ② 料炒勻成麵糊，淋於白菜上。
4　烤箱預熱至220℃(425°F)，烤盅置上層，烤約15分鐘至表面呈金黃色即可。

老師的叮嚀：
1　此道菜可先煮好放烤盅，存在冰箱，於食前再入烤箱加熱並烤上色即可。
2　焗至表面上色之菜餚宜置於烤箱上層或以上火烤。

2⅔ lb. (1200g) nappa
　　cabbage
2 ham slices or 2½ oz. (75g)
　　lean pork
①「1½ t. salt, 2c. stock
　└1t. sugar
5T. butter
½ c. minced onions
5T. flour
②「2½ c. juice of cooked
　　cabbage
　└½ c. condensed evaporated
　　milk

1　Rinse nappa cabbage and cut into chucks. Blanch in boiling water (put in stems first) until soft; remove.
2　Heat 3T. oil and stir-fry ham. Add nappa cabbage to stir-fry. Add ① and cook for about 5 minutes; remove and drain (save the juice for later use). Put the cabbage and ham in a baking casserole.
3　Heat butter over low heat and stir-fry onions until soft. Add flour and stir-fry until fragrant. Add in ② gradually and stir-fry to form a thick paste; remove. Pour over cabbage.
4　Preheat oven to 220℃ (425°F). Bake nappa cabbage on upper rack for 15 minutes until golden brown on the surface; serve.

Footnotes:
1　Nappa cabbage may be cooked in advance and put in a baking casserole, then refrigerated; before serving, reheat in oven to achieve a golden brown hue.
2　Bake foods over upper heat or on upper rack to achieve a golden brown surface.

烤芋薯
Baked Potatoes

蕃薯或馬鈴薯或芋頭2個
………… 約900公克 (1½斤)

① ┌ 水 ……………………… 6杯
   └ 鹽 ……………………… 1大匙

1 將芋薯放在 ① 料內浸泡約30分鐘後取出。

2 烤箱預熱至 200℃ (400°F)，芋薯放烤架上，置中層烤約1小時至軟，以筷子可輕易插入即成。

老師的叮嚀：

1 芋薯泡過鹽水除了可加速烤熟外，且帶有淡淡的鹹度，味更香。

2 烤芋薯時不包鋁箔紙味道較香，且自己在家烤非常方便。

---

2 potatoes, sweet potatoes, or taros, 2lb. (900g)

① ┌ 6c. water
   └ 1T. salt

1 Soak potatoes or taros in ① for about 30 minutes; remove.

2 Preheat oven to 200°C (400°F). Bake potatoes or taros on middle rack for about 1 hour until they become soft and are easily pierced through by a fork; serve.

Footnotes:

1 Soaking potatoes or taros in salty water will reduce the baking time and enhance flavor.

2 Baking potatoes or taros without wrapping in foil paper will increase aroma.

創意燒烤

索　引

Creative Chinese Oven Cooking
INDEX